Acclaim for *Outsell Your Co*
by Robin Fielder

'*Outsell Your Competition* is truly packed with sales tips and winning "how to's". I immediately ordered 200 copies for my National Sales Management Team. A compulsive read.'
Ian Stuart, Director of Network Sales, Lombard

'This book is an inspiration – as alive and powerful as being face to face with the author himself. If you can't get in front of him, I recommend you get this book in front of you.'
Mike Ketley, Senior Director, Yamaha-Kemble Music

'Comprehensive, visionary, incisive. I counted ten, value-loaded sales lessons in just the first three pages! Peppered with real-life examples that show these ideas really work, Robin has created a "must have" for every sales professional.'
Grant Cullen, Head of Sales Training, Virgin Direct

'This has to be one of the most up-to-date and outstanding sales guides which I have had the privilege of reading. Robin has catalogued a variety of easy-to-follow tips which, when applied in the sales arena, will really make the difference. As I turned each page, I found myself saying yes, yes in agreement. I couldn't put it down!'
Dennis Carton, Retail Director
UK Business Development, NatWest Bank

'No matter how much you know, you will learn something new from Robin Fielder's excellent new book, every page is packed with practical, powerful ideas and strategies that if applied correctly cannot fail to help you win more business. I review many books on the profession of selling and rarely do you find one that defines, clarifies and explains all aspects of the sales process in such a fast-moving, clear and useable way. If you want to learn how to sell more, read this book'
Adrian Tripp,
Publishing Editor of *Winning Business* Magazine and
Chief Executive of the *National Sales Awards*

(continued overleaf)

'If you want to learn how to sell, read this book. If you want to learn how to survive as well, read Part 4 again – and make notes! This will teach the inexperienced what they need to know, and remind the experienced what they may have forgotten. An excellent insight into our profession.'

Trevor Nichols,
UK Sales Director, Diagnostic Division,
Abbott Laboratories

'Everything you need to know about modern professional selling skills is contained within the pages of this book. Whether you're new to sales or have years of experience it is packed with inspiring ideas.'

Mark Reynolds, Corporate Sales Director,
Majestic Wine Warehouse

'Robin Fielder has really kept pace with the massive changes that are taking place in selling and sales management. In *Outsell Your Competition* he has managed to take a complex subject and distil it into a series of readily identifiable processes. The book is full of things the reader can actually *do* that will help him or her keep ahead of the competition.'

Patrick Joiner, Chief Executive,
The Institute of Sales & Marketing Management

'If you only get to take advice in selling from one person then make sure that it is Robin Fielder. He is, without doubt, the number one authority in the country on selling and personal performance.'

Jeff Dale, Sales Director, CD Sales Recruitment

'For those determined to be outstandingly successful, whether selling products, services or even ideas, this is a unique and innovative guide to becoming a resource valued by customers, using the latest techniques and written by an author who has been a winner throughout his career.'

Richard Mellor, General Manager,
Europe/Africa Trades, P&O Nedlloyd

'Robin Fielder's sales training courses crackle with energy and excitement, but they are also highly informative. It's no surprise then that his first book is a corker. My advice to anyone who sells, manages sales or wants to sell is: buy, read, act.'

Duncan Movassaghi, Regional Sales Manager, Halifax Bank of Scotland

'Robin Fielder is not only inspirational on his feet but he is also able to make an impact through the written word. *Outsell Your Competition* is relentlessly positive and *practical*. I look forward to reading the book again and again.'

Helena Boschi, Head of Global Organisation Development, Serono International SA

'Very straightforward and simple, everything you need to know to be a successful salesperson.'

Frank Emerson, Managing Director, ENG

'Robin Fielder brings his effervescent presentation style into print in this must have publication. Every page contains practical and well thought out methods to help anyone in sales, business and in life. If you only read one book this year make sure it is this one.'

Stuart Small, Vice President of European Sales & Support, OneSource Information Services

'*Outsell Your Competition* is a fantastic read. The focus on consultative-partnering takes the relationship one stage further, impactful examples show you exactly what to do, and anecdotes really bring the material alive.'

Marion Gray, Deputy Head of Business Banking, The Royal Bank of Scotland

For all those who aspire to be winners but most of all for Lucy, Tom and Lexi, the three most talented salespeople I have ever met.

Outsell Your Competition

Consultative selling strategies for the 21st century

Robin Fielder

THE McGRAW-HILL COMPANIES

London · Burr Ridge IL · New York · St Louis · San Francisco
Auckland · Bogotá · Caracas · Lisbon · Madrid · Mexico · Milan
Montreal · New Delhi · Panama · Paris · San Juan · São Paulo
Singapore · Sydney · Tokyo · Toronto

Published by McGraw-Hill Professional
Shoppenhangers Road
Maidenhead
Berkshire
SL6 2QL
Telephone: 44 (0) 1628 502 500
Fax: 44 (0) 1628 770 224
Website: www.mcgraw-hill.co.uk

Sponsoring Editor: Elizabeth Robinson
Editorial Assistant: Sarah Wilks
Marketing Manager: Elizabeth McKeever
Senior Production Manager: Max Elvey

Produced for McGraw-Hill by Steven Gardiner Ltd
Text design by Steven Gardiner Ltd
Printed and bound in Great Britain by Bell and Bain Ltd, Glasgow
Cover design by Senate Design Ltd

McGraw-Hill

A Division of The McGraw·Hill Companies

British Library Cataloguing in Publication Data
A catalogue record for this book is available from the British Library

Library of Congress Cataloguing in Publication Data
The Library of Congress data for this book has been applied for from the
Library of Congress

ISBN 0 07 709937 0

McGraw-Hill books are available at special quantity discounts. Please contact
the Corporate Sales Executive at the above address

**RACERNI, LACPOMAC & LACPAAC are registered trademarks of
Leadership Development Holdings Ltd, London, England**

Contents

Part Two: Buying and Selling

Part Three: Selling Skills

Part Four: Personal Skills

Acknowledgements

Special thanks to:
Alison Ridler, Nick Evans, Julian Feinstein, Nicki Fox, Richard Morley, David Marsh, Robin Lines, Catherine Kenny, David Harman, Kirsten Hannah, Tim French, Catherine Fielder, Rachel Walker-Keller, Michelle Tempest, Courtney Ferguson, Sally Lansdell, Liz Chambers and Elizabeth Robinson – as well as all those aspiring men and women who have attended my seminars and courses over the years from whom I've learned so much.

They all deserve to have their names up in lights for their contributions, either directly or indirectly, towards making this book possible.

About the Author

Robin Fielder is founder and CEO of Leadership Development Ltd (LDL), one of the UK's foremost business training providers.

A science graduate with a BSc in electronics from Southampton University, he began his career in the electronics industry. He then moved successfully into the world of selling, achieving more in five years than most people do in twenty.

In 1974, after breaking the individual sales record of one company within six months of joining, he decided to form LDL.

LDL was started with the express purpose of combining well-researched, tried and tested, up-to-the-minute skills training with personal development.

As head of LDL, Robin has personally conducted over 800 seminars to 250,000 executives in the last twenty years. His seminars on sales, leadership, negotiation, personal development and success psychology draw capacity audiences wherever he appears. He is the author of the Close That Sale! Seminar series (127,000 delegates so far make this programme the biggest-selling seminar in UK training history), Negotiate to Win, Big Ticket Selling, Professional Selling Skills, Professional Sales Management, Major Account Selling, Effective Speaking and Presentation, Towards Peak Performance and Inspirational Leadership.

A dynamic and exciting speaker, he has the uncanny knack of reducing business skills into a series of easy-to-follow steps and then getting his audience to use them. His dynamic approach, his drive, his enthusiasm transmits itself to participants and never fails to influence them.

He is married with three children, lives in Chelsea and is a keen sailor in his spare time. If you are interested in having Robin Fielder

speak to your organisation please telephone +44(0) 20 7381 6233
or email training@ldl.co.uk or visit us at www.ldl.co.uk.

Leadership Development Ltd
495 Fulham Road
London SW6 1HH

Introduction

Selling is changing because business is changing. Product and positioning no longer confer market advantage, because almost anything can be copied. In addition, customers are more knowledgeable and have more choices than ever before.

So how do you differentiate your business? How do you outsell your competition?

Salespeople used to learn about their product or service, its features and benefits, how to make presentations, sell value, handle objections and close. Then they targeted potential customers and went for the sale. But this approach now works in fewer and fewer cases. It has become superseded by a new, more effective way of selling.

The new role of the salesperson is to help customers improve and develop their own businesses – to be perceived as a source of value *in addition to* the product or service they supply. Selling is no longer just 'What are your requirements and how can we meet them?' – now it's 'Where are you going and how can we help you get there?'.

The twenty-first-century salesperson is a specialist, a problem solver and a relationship manager. The overriding objective is to become a valued resource to the customer rather than just someone who sells. In fact, if all you do is attempt to sell your products and services you're in danger of becoming a dinosaur. Personal selling in this fast forward, wired marketplace requires a new mindset - you need to be *in* business with your customers, not just *doing* business with them. The acid test is to ask yourself whether your customer would still hire you as a consultant if you no longer had your product or service to sell. This approach – part consultant, part partner – is called consultative-partner selling, and is discussed in detail in Part I of this book.

Traditionally sales training focuses on the steps the seller takes in making the sale, but people buy using *their* buying pattern not our sales pattern. To sell effectively it is vital to understand the steps the buyer moves through in making a purchase. Therefore Part II investigates the psychology behind buying using the RACERNI® buying sequence.

Clarity is key. The successful consultative-partner seller has a clear, clean understanding of the psychology of selling. Part II includes details of a four-step selling sequence based on the simple yet powerful concept of find out and match. The concept of 'people buy people first and whatever else second' is equally gaining in importance as companies realise that they need on-going relationships with their customers. This has major implications for the development of the right kind of selling skills. The most pivotal skills are covered in Part III, ranging from prospecting to major account selling. Further skills are covered in appendices I and II.

Competitive advantage, moreover, is not only about sales skills – it's about drive, confidence and invincible determination. In business as in sport, *the skill to win must be matched by the will to win.* Athletes call it mental toughness training. What really matters is how you run your mind. If it's good enough for Olympic champions, how about you?

Every industry has its sales superstars, people who reach heights that amaze and confound their colleagues. No matter what the economy does or where the newspapers say their industries are headed, they perform. Their trademark is consistency. They work on themselves, they learn their craft, they apply what they learn. And above all, they train themselves to be mentally strong. Like everyone else they experience setbacks and moments of self-doubt, but they don't allow such things to hold them back. Part IV will help you understand the personal skills and attitude you need to outsell your competition.

I urge you to read this section again and again, especially when you feel challenged by a stretch goal.

We all sell differently and, at the end of this book, I still want you to sell in your own unique way. Selling is not an exact science. There is no ideal, catchy, all-purpose way of selling. The secret is to be yourself – no tricks, no smoke and mirrors, just you at your best. What this book provides is processes and insights to help you uncover information, build relationships, develop yourself and stay ahead of the competition.

As you complete each chapter, make the material yours. Analyse the ideas, take them apart and mould them to fit you. That's where the real value lies.

Part One
THE SELLING CONCEPT

∎
Selling the Difference

As much as you want the business, so does someone else

How do you differentiate your company and your products and services in an increasingly competitive market? How do you ensure that customers buy from you rather than from your competitors? If a customer asks why they should buy from you, most salespeople respond with something like, 'We've got the best product, the best service, the best terms, buy from us.' But your competitors would say exactly the same! Customers *know* we think our product or service is the best – what they want to know is *why*.

Selling against competition is about selling the difference. Can you say what's special about your company, your product or service? What does your organisation do that makes you proud to work there? What can you offer the customer that your competitors can't?

▶ Your Relationship is a USP

Traditionally, salespeople have focused on USPs – unique selling points, reflecting what is different or special about your offering. They exist in three areas: your *product*, your *organisation* and *you*.

USPs answer the following questions:

- Why do people buy from us?
- Why do people buy from our competitors?

Analysing the answers to these questions will enable you to identify what the differences are and therefore the benefits your USPs offer to your customers.

Product USPs, often referred to as hard differentiators, are the ones we instinctively talk about. They are quantifiable: price, speed, compatibility, maintenance, technical specifications, quality. It is relatively easy to sell on the basis of product differentiators: if you have the lightest laptop on the market, for example, uncover a concern in that area and build on the value of lightness. However, once a market becomes hot, it attracts a plethora of wannabes. Competitors arrive, all offering the same or similar features, and your advantage disappears.

- Kevin Bohren of Compaq says, 'It used to be when we launched a new product it had six months of uniqueness, now it's a long weekend.'
- In January 1986 there were 12 IBM PC clones. By January 1987 there were 200.
- Peter Wood created Direct Line Insurance, offering customers the opportunity to buy personal insurance direct by phone. Initially the company made stunning profits and so attracted competitors. There are now over 50 UK-based companies offering telephone insurance.
- 0800 customer service hotlines were once seen as adding value and commanding a price premium. They are now an expected part of a company's service package.
- Federal Express started with a great differentiator: overnight delivery. Now there's TNT, UPS, DHL, Parcelforce and others. Overnight delivery is no longer a unique sales point, it's a commodity.

The advent of global communications means that just about anything can be produced anywhere. Products can be copied and services replicated. What gave us competitive advantage yesterday is a commodity offered by everyone today. So how do you differentiate your offering? What can you rely on to win?

Neil Flett trained the Australian team that sold the International Olympic Committee (IOC) on the benefits of holding the year 2000 games in Sydney. That sale was worth about US$7 billion to Australia in TV rights, licensing and tourism. There were four other finalists for the Olympic bid: Manchester, Beijing, Istanbul and Berlin.

Allegations of corruption aside, Flett's comments on what must be the ultimate competitive sale in the real world are worth noting. 'You must have clarity of purpose at all times,' he says. 'Big account selling is the art of listening someone into a sale. To build a foundation of support, you need to know who's a decision maker and who's an influencer, as well as their rationale, emotional and political values.'

The Sydney team built an exact replica of the final presentation venue in Monte Carlo, down to the top table, the speaker's table and screens, so that its presentation would be perfectly choreographed.
'When clients tell me they haven't got time to rehearse,' notes Flett, 'it's usually a reflection of their lack of intention to win. Like a good actor, the presenter has to rehearse his material until it is no longer a matter of memory but of genuine devotion to the message.'

Rehearsal is crucial even for small sales and negotiations, yet few sellers take the time to do this.

Think about the questions you're going to ask. Where's the customer coming from? Prepare for the way you intend to conclude. Consider what an acceptable negotiated agreement would be. How are you going to support or back up your position?

For larger sales you will almost certainly be asked to make a formal presentation of your proposals to the buying team. The most important element here, as always, is to focus on the customer. However, without proper preparation, the seller can be so focused on getting the words right that customer reactions are missed.

In the best-run sales teams rehearsals for key presentations occur without fail. Rehearse after work, at weekends, at midnight or at 6am – whenever and wherever suits you.

Rehearsal is fundamental to winning.

'I never make a shot, not even in practice, without first having a very clear in-focus picture of it in my head.'

Jack Niklaus, golfer

▶ Building a Partnership

There are three main ways in which buyers and sellers do business.

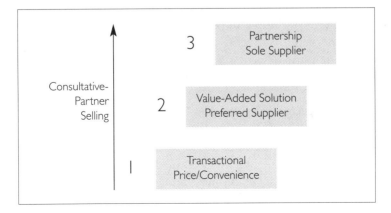

1. **Transactional.** The buyer perceives the product/service as a commodity that can be obtained from many providers and buys on the basis of price and convenience. Intense competition allows buyers to drive prices down, eroding sellers' margins. The cost of switching suppliers is low. Salespeople may no longer be affordable and accounts are serviced instead by telesales, call centres and the Internet.
2. **Value-added solutions.** Suppliers no longer sell products and services, they sell solutions. Salespeople are trained as problem solvers. Customers want to work with specialists in their own field. The salesperson is positioned as a consultant and profit improver. Many of today's sales relationships are in this category and the seller has the status of preferred supplier.
3. **Partnership.** The attitude taken under this approach is: 'Forget that we are two separate companies, what would we do if we were just one company?' Supplier and customer evolve a completely new way of working together, where it is difficult to see where one company ends and the other begins. The focus is on collaboration and on working together to drive cost out of the system, which results in lower prices and higher margins, so both parties benefit. The seller is the sole supplier and competitors are effectively locked out.

Partnership is the ideal to which many companies are striving, especially fast-track organisations such as those in technology, logistics and professional services. The more we can move towards this ultimate form of competitive advantage, the stronger and more durable our relationships with major accounts will become.

Partnering offers a glimpse of the future of account development. Customers are discarding rafts of suppliers in favour of the well-chosen few and developing close ties with them. By some estimates, companies have a third fewer suppliers than 10 years ago.

- Ford has reduced the number of suppliers it deals with from 52,000 to 5,000, a 90 per cent reduction.
- IBM made headlines in the *Wall Street Journal* with a stunning announcement: it was firing 40 advertising agencies and placing all its business with one agency, a $500 million switch.

Lou Pritchett, the former Vice-President of World-wide Sales at Procter & Gamble, is generally accepted as the pioneer of the partnering concept.

Wal-Mart was Procter & Gamble's largest customer. In his book *Stop Paddling & Start Rocking the Boat,* Pritchett writes, 'It's hard to believe, but no top corporate officer of Procter & Gamble had ever contacted any top corporate officer at Wal-Mart . . . I found that there was no sharing of information between the two companies. There was no joint planning, there was no systems co-ordination or compatibility. All there was were two separate corporate entities going their own ways, burdened by, but oblivious to, the excess costs that were being created by this obsolete system.'

Lou contacted Sam Walton and arranged a now famous canoe trip on the south fork of the Spring River in Hardy, Arkansas, so they could talk business away from the office. They agreed to collaborate with each other to create not Procter & Gamble's vision, nor Wal-Mart's vision, but a *mutual* vision, aiming to achieve goals that would benefit them both. Within a few months, the two companies had created a joint working group. Procter & Gamble brought in representatives from sales, marketing, systems, manufacturing, distribution and finance, to devise new ways of doing business with their counterparts at Wal-Mart. Lou Pritchett emphasises, 'Partnering is more than just playing golf and having lunch with people and hoping that your volume will increase and theirs will too. What it really is, is getting in and instead of having two dual, unconnected, incompatible systems, it's becoming extensions of each other's operations. Not to make you feel better, not to make the other company feel better, but to drive costs out of the system and deliver a better value to the end using customer.'

▶ Four Principles of Consultative Partnering

So companies at the leading edge of selling are concentrating on the one factor their competitors cannot copy – the business relationship they have with their customers. As product USPs become diluted, relationship issues, often called soft differentiators, are the main source of competitive advantage. Many businesses have realised that it is easier and more cost effective to sell more to existing accounts than to be continually searching for new ones.

By some estimates, boosting a company's customer retention rate by 2 per cent has the same effect on profits as cutting costs by 10 per cent. Companies such as Xerox, Sears, Toyota and General Electric have altered their compensation structures and now remunerate salespeople for thinking long term and working to retain customers.

Want a scenario to focus the mind? Imagine your business in five years' time. Assume you have six new competitors all offering the exact same product at a similar price. These organisations have set up in your vicinity and market themselves in a similar way. Competition is massive. Consider for a moment – how would you keep your customers? What's important?

The relationship is everything – there's nothing else. And here's the scary part: soft differentiators are very perishable, very fragile and fluid. So you've got to nurture the relationship to keep it alive and fresh.

> 'Your toughest competitors are your biggest allies. They're the ones who make you work harder, move faster and think smarter. They test your nerves, test your patience and try your ingenuity.'
>
> Dennis Conner, Americas Cup yachtsman

The twenty-first-century salesperson is a specialist, a problem solver and a relationship manager. This approach – part consultant, part partner – describes what I call the consultative-partner selling style.

The overriding objective is to become a valued resource to the customer. There are four principles to concentrate on when you are moving towards consultative partnering. Master these and you will transform your approach to important sales opportunities.

▶ The First Principle: Bring More to the Table than Just a Sale

Look energetically for ways to be a resource to your customers. The language of modern selling is not: 'What do you require and how can we sell it to you?' It is: 'Where are you going and how can we help you get there?'

What could your organisation offer to help your customers run their businesses more effectively? Could you help your best customers reduce cost without reducing your price? What else can you offer in addition to your solution?

- A recruitment company supplies clients with industry-specific salary details to help them plan future employment policy.
- A stationer becomes stock controller and distributor for its major customers' standard stationery items.
- A cable manufacturer helps customers cut inventory by providing online access to its price lists and stockholding.
- Car leasing firms offer their clients information on fuel consumption, diesel vs petrol, maintenance, accidents and resale values to help them improve the management of their fleets.
- A supplier of industrial controls provides customers with online information on the 6,000 products it offers.

Never underestimate the importance of value-added services in creating partner relations.

Initiatives such as these have one main objective: to increase the customer's cost of switching suppliers. The higher the cost of switching, the less likely it is to happen.

At every opportunity ask yourself, 'How much would it cost my best customer to switch to the competition? *How can I increase this cost?*' Bring more to the table than just your products and services.

The object is to become indispensable to your customer and so create 'barriers to entry' for your competitors and 'barriers to exit' for your customers. Put yourself in your customer's shoes and ask, 'What would I lose if I lost this supplier?' If the answer is 'not much', you're doing the job wrong.

▶ The Second Principle: Want the Business

This sounds obvious, but it is much deeper than it appears. When we are dealing directly with buyers, we have to learn how to sell ourselves effectively. Giving your customer the impression you really want *their* business can be very persuasive.

Think about your own experiences. Time and again if people have gone to great lengths to make you feel important and valued, you choose a supplier based on that feeling, not just on the proposed solution.

Here is an example:

One of my colleagues at LDL, Robin Lines, works with a client called Bonas Machine Tools in Gateshead. The company won a £1 million contract to supply a German customer against very strong competition from the market leader, who was apparently prepared to discount strongly to get the business. The contract took a year to negotiate and finalise.

Bonas's MD, Ian Harris, phoned the German customer and asked, 'I'm delighted we've won, may I ask you why you have given us the contract?' The customer replied, 'For one reason, we felt you were hungrier, more energetic. At the end of the day, we paid more for you but we felt you were going to be more responsive, more flexible.'

Imagine you are interviewing candidates for an important position. You have drawn up a final shortlist of two people, John and David. John is slightly better qualified than David, but David really wants the job. Who would you offer it to? We have asked this question to thousands of managers over the years and the vast majority answer 'David'.

It's exactly the same in business: we want to do business with people who make us think they will look after us, who convince us they really want to work together. John Hegarty, Creative Director of the BBH Advertising Agency which created the Levis 501 and Haagen-Daz campaigns, puts it this way: *'People want to do business with people who pay attention to them.'* That says it all.

Suppose your managing director passed you a lead and said, 'This is the only lead you are allowed to deal with in the coming 12 months. What you do with it will determine how much we pay you and what your promotion prospects are.'

How would you handle that lead? You would give the customer the benefit of your personal attention. To succeed, treat each lead as if it were the only one.

The impression you want to create is: 'You can't buy anything from my company without getting me with it: my help, my assistance, my back-up, me on the end of the phone.' 'You have my personal guarantee this will be installed on time. I promise you, you'll look back on this conversation and think it was one of the best decisions you've ever made.'

Put these phrases into your own style and be confident about using them with clients.

▶ The Third Principle:
Use Team Selling

The more people from both supplier and customer who are involved in building the relationship, the stronger it becomes. It's a team effort. When your team meets the customer and explains what each member does, it gives you more credibility. The customer appreciates having access to all the players. They know who is going to carry out each element of servicing the account.

It's no longer just the account manager talking with the buyer, it's the supplier team working with the customer team to optimise effectiveness. And from the buyer's perspective, the more people involved in the relationship, the harder it is to change supplier. They would need to be satisfied that all their key people had no objection to the change.

All contact with a customer should be coordinated through the Account Manager, who ensures that the account objectives are clear to all concerned and acts as team leader. The overall objective is to ensure that all the supplier's resources – sales, support marketing, research, finance, packaging and distribution – are used to identify and meet the customer's requirements profitably for both parties.

When organising a team you shouldn't be thinking: 'How can I put the best team together to win the business?' Instead, focus on: 'Who needs to be involved so we can bring in all the expertise we've got to help the customer achieve their objective?'

Everyone in the company, from product designers to factory managers to financial officers to service managers, must be involved in selling to and servicing the customer. In the best-run companies, all employees are salespeople. Engineers, designers, production managers and scientists can benefit enormously from learning selling skills.

Top management should also be involved. CEOs must visibly lead in partnership selling by acting as salesperson-in-chief.

▶ The Fourth Principle:
Focus on the Customer's Customer

What happens when a new business proposal comes into your office? For most of us this signals a determined effort to beat the competition. We seek to entice the new customer or client with better product value, better service, better proposals and a strong desire for them to just plain like us more than our competitors.

Top salespeople go further than this and ask:

- 'What do my customers require to satisfy *their customers?*', and
- 'Who are *their competitors* and how can we help them to win?'

The golden rule of business – I can get what I want by helping others get what they want – is best applied by thinking about both your customer's customer and your customer's competitor.

Intel's brilliant 'Intel Inside' marketing campaign worked because the chip maker looked not only at its own customers – OEMs and distributors – but at *their* customers, the man or woman looking for a new PC. Never before has the end user been so aware of the brand identity of a single component.

Once again, this approach is about understanding the customer, about being a specialist and a consultant in their business. You need to understand what causes their profits to go up and down. What gets them excited? What business are they in? Who are their competitors? Why do they win business? Why do they lose business? How do they make money? What are their major costs? Where are they going?

▶ The Basics of Selling the Difference

As companies move from a transactional to a relationship focus in their dealings with customers, the concept of *'people buy people first and whatever else second'* gains in importance every day. There are five basic points you should keep in mind when face to face with a prospective customer or client.

- **Wherever possible, never mention your competitors by name.** This is free advertising and it simply raises the customer's confidence in your competition. Many salespeople make this mistake, so be careful. By all means talk about the competition, but not by name. Instead, refer to them as 'other' companies or 'other' suppliers.
- **Wherever possible, don't talk about your competitors at all.** Just because you're in a competitive market, don't always assume that you are up against competition. If you ask your customer if they are seeing anyone else, they might think they should. Instead, in order to test whether or not you are up

against competition, ask: 'Have you done anything about this so far?' or 'How far have you got with this?' or 'What plans have you got for solving this situation?'

■ **If you must talk about them, don't say 'our competitors' or 'the competition' or 'compare us with'.** All these phrases simply add credibility to the strength of your so-called competition. If someone asks you who your competitors are – a perfectly reasonable question for an intelligent executive to ask – be positive and a touch humorous and answer: 'I don't know, we haven't got any. There are a number of other companies in the same business as us. There are even some who have products with a similar name, but that's where the similarity ends because . . .' And then accentuate the *difference*, sell the difference.

■ **Don't knock your competitors.** Knocking is unprofessional and amateurish. It also breaks the basic rule of business – what you hand out, you get back. However, nor should you get too carried away with praise. Remember the rule – pay the highest compliment to the least likely contender! Praise will also work well against competition should they choose to speak badly of you. And remember that no knocking doesn't necessarily mean not pointing out their weaknesses or drawbacks. It means not saying nasty, unpleasant things about them: don't criticise their products, services or staff and don't condemn what they do.

■ **Concentrate on your strengths.** Make sure your customer knows why you think your product or service is better and what that means. Don't be overly concerned about what you can't do, instead concentrate on what you *can* do. Sell your strengths.

▶ Selling the Difference Summary of Main Points

■ Selling against competition is about selling the difference. You have to give your customer solid reasons to choose you.

■ Recognise that hard differentiators become eroded when competitors arrive offering similar features.

■ Soft differentiators or relationship issues are vital. As products and services become more and more alike, the quality of the relationship becomes *the* deciding factor.

- Be a partner. Move towards the ultimate relationship. Forget that you are separate companies, what would you do if you were just one company?
- Bring more to the table than just a sale. Do everything to increase your customer's cost of switching suppliers. Think about being *in* business with them, not *doing* business with them.
- Want the business. Communicate your intention to win. Let the customer sense you are hungry for the business.
- Use team selling. It's no longer the account manager talking with the buyer, it's the supplier team working with the customer team.
- Focus on the customer's customer. What do your customers require to satisfy *their* customers?

2
Selling Solutions

Be a consultant. Move beyond features and benefits and ask what you can solve for the customer.

Since time immemorial, converting features into benefits has been ground zero for sales skills. But it's no longer enough. Your customers have heard it all before and they've stopped listening.

Customers no longer want to talk to salespeople, they want to talk to problem solvers. This means extending your horizon beyond selling products and services. As we saw in Chapter 1, to succeed you must understand your customer's business and be able to identify the problems they are experiencing and the solutions they might find attractive *before* offering your assistance.

Some years ago, faced with falling profits, CEO of Digital Equipment Ken Olsen admitted: 'We've been selling computers while what our customers want are solutions to their business problems.'

Think about it: the CEO of what was then one of the world's largest computer companies was attributing his company's disappointing performance to the fact that his salesforce were selling his company's products and services.

He knew that what they should be doing was selling *how* they could solve their customers' problems, *how* they could boost the productivity of their customers' factories and offices. Selling solutions is what being a consultant is all about.

■ Before Microsoft, IBM was king of the computer industry. Then it collapsed as its mainframe business slowed and its newer products were copied. Today it is re-emerging, not as a product-led company, but as a solutions consultancy.

■ Fmcg (fast moving consumer goods) suppliers are chosen on the basis of their ability to supply retail expertise, not on the quality of their products. Knowledge of how to compete for customers is seen as the valuable resource.

■ The head of Revlon famously said that women spend millions on cosmetics, but it's not cosmetics they want. In its factories Revlon makes cosmetics, but in the shops it helps solve the problems of ageing by selling hope, youth and beauty.

Competition has shifted from who has the best products to who can best improve the customer's operations. The best salespeople focus on real business issues. They help their customers not only to solve problems but also to avoid future problems by anticipating changes in market conditions. *They sell from the customer's perspective rather than their own.*

▶ Selling or Solving?

To focus your approach, think of a sale you're working on now and ask yourself, 'Am I attempting to sell my products and services or solve the customer's problems?'

If you hesitate before replying, don't worry, that's normal. Most people haven't thought about this before. And in case you're wondering, the approach applies to all sales, not merely the larger ones.

> A Canadian attempted to sell a Jeep that had a snow plough attachment. He ran several classified ads that mentioned new tyres, low mileage, good engine and so forth. No sale.
> Then he thought about selling solutions and ran the following ad in the Business Opportunities section: *Start your own snow removal business. Late model Jeep with plough. Excellent money-making potential.* The Jeep sold the first day.

Let's look at how you apply this concept to everyday sales situations.

A tried-and-tested method of improving your approach is to get into a 'What will it solve?' mindset. Before a sale, make a list of all the problems or potential problems you believe you can solve for your customer. You can do this alone or as a team exercise with colleagues at work. Keep this list at the forefront of your mind as the sale begins and you will automatically ask better questions. (Chapter 7 on gap analysis selling looks at this process in detail.)

If you're a sales manager, whether your sales are booming or your team are having difficulty meeting their targets, keep saying over and over: '**Help our customers to solve their problems.**' Be like a record stuck in a groove and you'll be rewarded with better sales.

▶ Five Insights into Consultative-Partner Selling

There are five insights essential to selling solutions, which will strengthen your approach to every sales opportunity.

1 – Be a Specialist

How would you react to being referred to a Harley Street doctor who claimed to be a leading authority on orthopaedics, gynaecology and ophthalmology? You'd run a mile from such obvious quackery. It's just not possible to be a master of all those disciplines.

Such a scenario is ridiculous, but salespeople often miss the underlying point. If you try to be all things to all people, you will be nothing to no one. Instead, be brilliant at the one subject closest to the customer's heart – their business.

When General Electric's largest customers were asked what they expected from a salesperson, they replied: 'The number one thing we expect is excellent knowledge of our company, our industry and the environment in which we do business.'

The more you specialise in an industry, the better sense you will have of the problems and opportunities there to be uncovered. Approach the account with: 'In this type of business, it often happens that this situation arises. Is that the case here?'

The biggest complaint customers have about salespeople is that they seem to know nothing about their business, nor do they attempt to learn much. The highest compliment your customer can pay you is, '*You understand our business.*' That means they regard you as a partner, not just as a mere vendor.

Frequently a potential customer will test your knowledge early in a meeting. He will ask you what you know about his industry or about some aspect that is currently concerning him. He wants to be reassured that you know what you're talking about and you are the sort of person he wants to do business with.

Don't disappoint him! This is your opportunity to demonstrate your expertise. Whenever you are tested, rise to the challenge and establish your credibility and knowledge. It's your entry to the sale.

'Spectacular achievement is always preceded by spectacular preparation.'

Robert Schuller, *Possibility Thinking*

The key question

So when we stand in front of an important customer, we must present *new* knowledge about improving their business. This leads us to a question that provides real insight into what's required to outsell your competition both now and in the future. Get it right and you will catapult yourself into the top 10 per cent of sellers.

- **Would your customer still hire you as a consultant if you no longer had your product or service to sell?**

I believe that this question, more than anything else, captures the essence of modern consultative-partner selling. The answer clearly reveals whether you are a resource to the customer or merely a person who sells.

Take this on board. Work at it and I guarantee you will accelerate your achievement. Nothing, but nothing, will provide you with better insurance against turbulent markets and the ever-present threat of new competitors entering your market.

Boosting your knowledge

Here are some ideas to help you to arrive knowledgeable and stand out from the pack.

- **Do your homework.** Before your first meeting with the customer, do as much research as you can on the account. Search the customer's website. The Internet is the ultimate research tool. A webhead I'm not, but it beats me how we used to manage without it. Have printed pages from the site with you at the meeting so the customer can see you've come prepared – this is always impressive.
- **Read your customers' trade press.** Most of us read our own trade press, but we must also read that of our customers. This provides a feel for the problems, trends, opportunities and challenges of that industry. It helps you develop a sixth sense as to where the problems occur that your product/service will solve. It's one of the very best ways to learn about the industry to which you sell. You could also find out if there are any bulletin boards or trade websites aimed at this particular industry.
- **Choose an industry or vertical market to specialise in.** To be a top salesperson you have no choice, you must specialise.

- Kodak's high-speed copier salespeople know as much about operating a quick print copy shop as the franchise owners.
- IBM's 70,000-strong worldwide salesforce is divided into 14 speciality markets, such as travel, banking, insurance and pharmaceuticals.
- NCR knows as much about the retail environment as any retailer. It has worked, studied and analysed that niche for decades.

Your aim is to know more than anyone else, but this takes time so choose your target market carefully. Just like becoming a doctor, it's sometimes very hard to build up the necessary knowledge to get qualified – but it is always worth the effort.

- **From time to time read the financial press.** The language of business is money. Publications, such as the *Financial Times* and *Wall Street Journal* help you to feel familiar and more articulate with the subject. They also provides insights into which industries are growing and which are declining. Carry a copy with you and use any waiting time at airports, stations or reception areas to keep yourself up to date.
- **Join trade associations of target customers.** Some salespeople even take courses aimed at their user customers. Then they really understand their customer's concerns.

2 – Reduce Risk

Buying is a risky business. If you want to persuade customers to buy your solution, you must first convince them that the risk of doing so is low.

Salespeople often fear rejection, but the customer also has a fear – the fear of making a mistake, of paying too much, of being criticised for making the wrong choice, or of being left stranded by your company because the support is inadequate.

Reducing the perception of risk is a concept that should permeate all your selling. Position your company as the low-risk provider of the required solution. Demonstrate that doing business with you is the *safe option*.

How to sell safety

What do you think lowers risk in the customer's mind? It could be your company's reputation, stability, client base, quality awards, or having lots of satisfied customers. And if you have high repeat business, then be sure to talk about it.

Karen Zupko, a highly respected business consultant working with medical practitioners, has a great line: *'In God is all our trust – everyone else bring data.'*

Her point is right on the money. For the customer to trust you, you must provide evidence – the harder the better – that confirms the quality of your product or service.

This also means being careful of woolly claims such as 'It's cost effective'. You are unlikely to have been in a situation where a buyer heard that expression and said, 'Really, you're cost effective. That's incredible. Just what we want, because the supplier we're using now is cost hopeless!'

Instead, demonstrate what you mean by cost effective. For example, 'On the basis of a 10 per cent reduction in processing time, this new system will pay for itself in eight months.'

Build a file of testimonials

But what lowers risk the most – what you say or what your customers say? Your customers' opinions are hugely important in reducing the perception of risk, so use testimonials, case histories, client lists, references and reference sites wherever possible.

Direct marketers have long known the power of testimonials. By some estimates, if you create two direct mail pieces identical in every way except that one contains solid testimonials and the other does not, the mailing with proof will pull as much as *10 times the response of the other.*

Ten testimonials are better than two; 100 are better than 10. One business magazine reported a client who doubled response in three months by going from one page of testimonials to 16. Now they're going to a 64-page bound paperback.

As a first stage, build a file of testimonials and attach relevant ones to every proposal. You'll find that your sales go up as soon as you start using them. Include them in a section of your website so potential customers can see them when they are finding out about you.

If you currently don't have any testimonials, set a goal to get 10 in the next four weeks. Contact your customers and ask them for a letter explaining their experience of your products/service and support and describing the benefits they have received. Most customers are only too pleased to do this: it's all part of building good business relations.

If your customer asks, 'What do you want me to say?', be careful you don't fall into the trap of saying, 'I'll leave it to you.' If the testimonial is a hassle to write, they won't do it. Instead, offer some ideas to help them, preferably by asking questions such as: 'What is the biggest benefit you have received?' Rather than generic assurances that you give good service ahead of the competition, encourage your customers to describe a specific way you helped. The objective is to make the task of writing the testimonial as simple and as easy as possible.

> In my office we frame testimonial letters and hang them on the wall of our reception area – we're very proud of them.
> If you like this book and get value from it, I'd be delighted if you would write and tell me how you have used the ideas. There's still space on our wall and it would give me a tremendous buzz to hear how you have applied the material.

If you're a start-up with a new product or service, get testimonials from scientists, experts, trial groups and anyone else you've worked with.

Once you get in the habit of using testimonials, keep them up to date and relevant to your target audience.

3 – Believe in Your Solution

Belief is a spectacularly important differentiator and value builder. When we believe in what we're offering and why it's the best, this belief comes across in our presentation and is very persuasive. If we are convinced then we'll be able to convince others and vice versa. **Never, ever forget that people are more persuaded by your convictions than by your arguments.** I urge you to write that in big capitals and put it where you'll see it every day.

How to keep your edge

If I asked you whether you believe in the value of what you sell, I'm sure you would reply very positively. The trouble is, when we are involved with the same product or service week after week, month after month, year after year, our belief tends to become sterile. The fire and passion we once had are replaced by a merely intellectual belief.

It's not surprising that we begin to lose some of our enthusiasm and that all-important 'edge' over time. But when we lose appreciation for what we sell, it tends to affect our relationships with customers. That's why it is so critical to remind ourselves constantly of the value we offer. It helps to keep the 'wow' factor alive.

As a trainer and seminar leader, I've come across many examples of brand new salespeople with virtually no training who sell well. Why does this happen?

They *believe* in what they offer, they are passionate about it, there is an emotional intensity to what they do. If you ask them how come they are doing so well, they say: 'I just believe in my product, it's fantastic, if I don't sell to someone I feel I've done them a huge disservice – it's that good.'

Be careful of priceitis

There is a belief-damaging disease that sellers often catch affectionately known as *priceitis*. The symptoms are waking up one morning believing that what we sell is somewhat pricey. Be warned, priceitis is highly contagious, worse than chickenpox or flu. If you have an attack of it, most of the customers you speak to that day will catch it and you'll lose business on the price objection.

It's important to appreciate that, assuming the product or service is not genuinely overpriced, all sellers get priceitis from time to time – irrespective of what they sell and how it is priced.

The cure is simple: take time out to rebuild your belief. While this may sound like an opportunity to step back, it is not an excuse to take the morning off; just spend a few minutes each day reselling yourself on the value of the solutions you offer. The best way to achieve this is to remind yourself of your satisfied customers. Remind yourself of the value they received and the problems you helped solve. It will make your selling easier and more natural.

Make it a habit to reread your own customer testimonials regularly. You'll be impressed and reinspired.

4 – Use Questions not Reasons as Your Main Persuasive Tools

When I first started out in sales, I thought you had to have the gift of the gab. I was convinced you had to be a great talker to get people to buy from you; this bothered me because I didn't think I had those skills. Everyone now recognises that the old spray and pray, 'gift of the gab' approach has no place in modern selling. In fact, if you are a great talker and can't learn to bite your tongue, then maybe selling is not for you.

And yet there are still some salespeople who think that a successful presentation is a matter of putting their case logically. Their presentations are flawless, their logic superb, their evidence overwhelming. If they were barristers they would be at the top of their profession. But what they don't realise is that they're not selling – they're telling.

If we *tell* people why they should buy, if we give them all the logic, all the reasons why they should go ahead, and we do it with enthusiasm, we will make some sales, but those people would probably buy anyway. Whether we like the description or not, we are in the role of order taker.

Don't fall into the trap of spending too much time telling customers about your products/services and not enough time *asking* them about their requirements. While revelling in the plusses of your offering may be fun, collecting information is likely to be more worthwhile.

Never tell if you can ask

Selling's most useful credo is: 'Forget the tell and develop the ask.' Rather than tell your customer the relevant benefits of what you offer, change such statements into questions.

The most persuasive way of transferring your ideas is through questions. It's been said many times and I'll repeat it here: it's much easier to teach an introvert to ask questions than to teach an extrovert to shut up.

Get the feel of asking questions. Can you recall when you learned to ride a bicycle? It felt awkward attempting to balance and steer in the right direction, didn't it? But after a while, after repeatedly falling off, you eventually mastered it. Now you can ride without thinking, it comes easily.

This is how we learn. Initially it feels awkward and strange. Gradually this gives way to being able to do it naturally and comfortably.

A recurring theme of this book is the concept of transferring ideas through questions, not reasons. It may feel awkward initially, but keep at it and you'll find that asking questions becomes as easy as riding your bicycle. Resist the temptation to *tell* people what you can do for them. Instead, *ask* them what difference it would make. The best way to persuade is with your ears.

5 – Understand the (Almost Magical) Power of Positioning

Positioning means how you are perceived by your marketplace. Your most valuable asset is your reputation: it acts as a magnet for new business leads. Customers will choose you because of your reputation – that's the real value of fame.

Perception is everything. It's not the reality, it's the *perception* of reality that counts. Everything we do is either contributing to or detracting from the way the customer views us. Like a jigsaw, if one piece is missing, the whole picture is spoiled.

Corporate positioning

Have you ever considered what people say about your organisation before they meet you?

One of the unassailable laws of marketing is that we get the sort of business we are positioned for. Whatever you sell, pause for a moment and ask yourself this question: 'How is my company perceived by my customers?'

Your sales aids and brochures must be as good as the product. Advertising and PR must reflect a predetermined positioning. Everything counts – reputation, superb customer service, how the phone is answered, what's on your website. Everything you do is having a drip-drip effect on shaping the way your customer perceives you, so it must all be thought through from the beginning.

Unless you are in the marketing department or on the board, you don't have that much control of corporate positioning. What you do have 100 per cent control of is your personal positioning.

Personal positioning

How are *you* perceived? What do people say about you when you're not there? What would you like them to say?

We often ask this question to delegates attending courses. The answer is usually 'They're a great person.' While we all want to be liked, this kind of comment is not likely to help us penetrate an important account.

We studied personal positioning and found that there are three things major customers say about outstanding salespeople:

■ 'They really understand my business and my industry. I learn from them.' That's surely the greatest compliment a customer can pay.

■ 'They are helping me solve my problems/achieve my goals.'
■ 'They work for me, like an unpaid member of my own staff.'

Think about it – if customers say that about you, what's going to happen when a competitor tries to break into the account? You've got it made.

As products and services become more and more alike, the difference is in the salespeople who sell them. We must differentiate ourselves. Constantly ratchet up your effectiveness by asking yourself how you can be recognised as the most capable in your field.

Why not write an article for your trade press? I know it's easier said than done, but that's what stretching ourselves is all about. Motivate yourself by thinking what it would do for your personal credibility. Always be asking, 'What can I do that goes above the norm?'

▶ Selling Solutions
Summary of Main Points

Customers no longer want to talk to salespeople, they want to talk to problem solvers. Have the attitude: I'm not in selling, I'm in problem solving.

There are five key insights essential to selling solutions.

■ *Be a specialist* – Everyone wants to deal with the person with the best knowledge. Would your customer still hire you as a consultant if you no longer had your product or service to sell? That question may seem hard to live up to, but the more you move in that direction the better your sales will be.

■ *Reduce risk* – Demonstrate that doing business with you is the low-risk option. Recognise the power of testimonials.

■ *Believe in your solution* – Always remember, people are more persuaded by your conviction than by your arguments. Work at keeping your belief alive.

■ *Use questions not reasons as your main persuasive tools* – Never tell if you can ask. Resist the temptation to *tell* people what you can do for them. Instead, *ask* them what difference it would make.

■ *Understand the power of positioning* – What do people say about you when you're not there? Give the customer the impression you work for them, not for your company. When it comes down to it, who pays your salary?

Part Two
BUYING AND SELLING

3

Psychology of the Buying Process

Boost your selling power by appreciating how the customer buys.

Have you ever tried to break a rock with your fist? That's what it's like attempting to penetrate an important account without an understanding of how the customer buys.

People not only buy what they want, they buy *in the way that they want*. Your role as a consultative-partner seller is to help them buy. And as the sale gets larger, such issues increase in importance.

▶ The RACERNI® Buying Sequence

So what does the buying process look like?

My colleagues and I embarked on an intensive investigation of how major purchases are made. We attended conferences, talked to senior managers and read everything we could find in books, journals and magazines on the subject of managing complex sales. It was an exciting and rewarding time. The output of this activity enabled us to identify seven distinct psychological stages through which a buyer moves.

These stages, outlined in full at the top of p. 32, can be described by the acronym RACERNI®:

Stage 1 – Recognise the Gap

What happens at the beginning of a purchase of any size? After thinking about their situation, the customer recognises a gap between what they are doing now and what they *could* be doing. That's how the sale begins.

On closer analysis, this gap takes one of two forms:

■ The customer becomes aware that there is a drawback/difficulty/concern with what they are doing at present; or

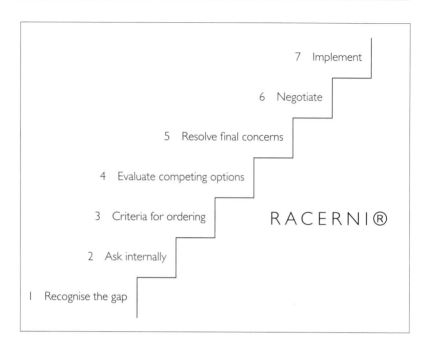

- The customer realises that there is an improvement that they could use to their benefit.

Once they have realised that a gap exists, the customer quickly moves to Stage 2.

Stage 2 – Ask Internally

The customer then asks themselves a crucial question: 'Is this gap large enough to justify action or are we happy to live with it?'

Their main focus is on whether this gap is worth the effort of doing something. Is this concern/drawback worth solving or devoting resources to? Is it worth their while taking advantage of this improvement?

And here's the challenge for you as a seller. If it's a major purchase, sooner or later someone in the account will step in and ask:

- How much is it costing us?
- How much more could we make?

Be aware that these are *quantified* concerns. The customer wants numbers because that's how they justify change inside their organisation. The salesperson who can help produce suitable numbers will be welcomed with open arms.

This is the time to use gap analysis skills (see Chapter 7). Work with the customer to widen the gap. Make the problem seem more serious and your solution seem more attractive.

A word of caution: if you work out how much the present situation is costing the customer and how much more could be made, you are likely to get the reaction, 'That's what *you* say.' As we've seen, the best approach is to sell *with* the customer not *to* them. Prepare your financial case jointly, as a team. It's not always straightforward in practice, but that's what you should aim for.

At this time, the decision makers in the organisation will almost certainly be discussing a ballpark level of funding. And, of course, they will also investigate what resources they have available themselves. The customer's first port of call when they need assistance is invariably their own resources. They will only consider going to the marketplace when no suitable internal resource exists, or internal resources are unavailable for some reason.

Once they recognise that there is indeed a gap that does need fixing, they move to Stage 3.

Stage 3 – Criteria for Ordering

The customer now draws up an initial specification based on what they perceive their requirements to be. This is then refined into written criteria for ordering, which can be circulated to potential suppliers.

This initial specification is usually in the form of a 'to do' list. The customer wants something that will do this . . . and this . . . and this . . . and this . . . The requirement is expressed in terms of a *solution*.

Many salespeople find it useful to help the customer construct the formal criteria by using the following three-step sequence.

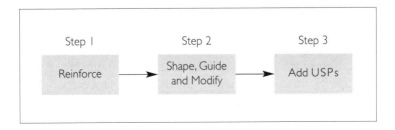

1. **Reinforce those requirements you can match**. If your customer has a requirement that your organisation is superb at matching, build up its importance by asking them to describe the benefits of having it.

   For example, if your customer says that the equipment to fill their perceived gap must have 'high operating speed' and that's one of your strong points, ask:

   ■ 'Why is that important?'
   ■ 'How will it help?'

   In explaining it to you the customer will reinforce it in their own mind. In this way the requirement becomes stronger.

2. **Shape, guide and modify**. If the customer brings up a requirement that you cannot match, then you should attempt to shape, guide and modify it, with their agreement, into one that you *can* match. (There is more on this skill in Chapter 4.)

   In effect, you use your objection-handling skills during **find out**, not **match**. Traditional sales techniques put objection handling at the end of the sale, but it doesn't matter how brilliantly an objection is dealt with, it still represents a question mark in the buyer's mind at that crucial time. New-style selling brings objection handling forward to the **ask** stage. The emphasis is on objection prevention, not cure.

3. **Add your USPs**. The objective of introducing USPs at this time is to build value in those areas that most differentiate you from your competitors. This helps to avoid the all too frequent trap of uncovering the requirement and selling the concept, but doing so in a way that allows a competitor to take the order.

   Consider what other requirements your customer should be thinking of in a purchase of this type. Introduce your ideas by way of questions. Rather than *tell* your customer what else you can do for him, rotate such statements into questions.

   For example, 'What about technical support? Would it be useful for you to have telephone access to the latest developments in printing materials and processes?'

   If the customer expresses interest, build on this by asking questions about why that aspect is important. What difference would it make? If there is no interest, simply go on to your next USP.

By refining the requirement and introducing your USPs, you establish a set of criteria that other suppliers will find it difficult to match. And always remember that your most compelling USP – and one your competitors will find it difficult to replicate – is the relationship you build with your customers.

As soon as the criteria for ordering are established, the foundation of the sale is complete. You can now present your proposals, carefully matching to each of the customer's requirements.

Let's assume that the presentation goes really well. You're feeling confident. The customer seemed to like you. Then you are hit with that dreaded phrase, 'Leave it with us, we'll get back to you.'

Even though your heart may sink, don't worry, this is normal. It's an important purchase and one of the ways the customer minimises the risk is to shop around. They have effectively moved to Stage 4.

Stage 4 – Evaluate Competing Options

The customer will now contact your competitors. They want to be sure they are making the right choice. Typically, they put together some sort of evaluation process such as a committee, with the brief to evaluate all the competing suppliers.

As a prospective customer, they usually do three things:

- Send out RFPs (requests for proposals).
- Evaluate incoming proposals against their criteria for ordering.
- Expect their criteria to be shaped, guided and modified by contact with the marketplace.

It is vital to recognise that at this stage the customer is focused on making the right choice. *Any salesperson who helps the customer to choose between suppliers is likely to have a great impact.*

I recall going into my office one Friday afternoon when we were evaluating competing options for hiring a PR agency. At this stage in the purchase we had decided we were going to proceed, but we were still considering which firm to use.

Our buying team had a shortlist of six agencies. Their concern was making the right choice.

I was walking past our conference room when the team emerged and seemed upset, in fact they were fuming. I asked what was wrong.

Their answer stopped me in my tracks. 'We've just wasted two hours in there with some account exec who's been talking us through why we should use PR. We know that! We've gone past that stage. We're annoyed as hell.'

That seller had made the all too common error of not considering where his customer was in the buying process. The customer was no longer thinking 'Shall we buy?' but 'Who shall we buy from?'

One approach you might use is to say, 'It's sometimes very confusing choosing between different suppliers. So we sat down and put together a list of eight questions (or however many you have) that we believe will be helpful to you in making the right choice, and we'd like to discuss them with you.'

You'll find your customer is delighted that you refrain from singing the praises of your own proposal and instead are offering to help them to choose between suppliers. This kind of approach has a professional feel to it that sets you apart from the pack.

The customer then moves to Stage 5 and the end game has started.

There is an old advertising story about the president of Young & Rubicam who, on hearing that the American Tobacco account was up for grabs, called that company's president and said, 'I hear you're looking for a new advertising agency. I have a number of questions that are helpful in choosing between agencies.'

On that basis he got an appointment. In fact, he didn't have the questions already, so he checked into a nearby hotel and asked himself, 'If I were the president of American Tobacco looking for a new agency, what questions would I want to ask that agency?'

After two days he came up with 12 questions.

At the appointment he reported up front what had happened. The American Tobacco president replied, 'I have a list as well – let's trade lists.' When he found that nine of the questions were the same on both lists, Young & Rubicam won the account, which they maintained for many years.

Stage 5 – Resolve Their Final Concerns

'Resolve their final concerns' isn't my description, it's Neil Rackham's, and it's a good one.

The customer is like a bridegroom before a wedding. They tend to get cold feet, they feel apprehensive – usually because someone elsewhere in their organisation has stepped in and asked questions like:

- What are the risks?
- Is this the right move for us?
- Are we going to get payback on this?
- How will our people respond?
- Do we really need all this aggravation at this time?

It's important to realise that customers don't always go through Stage 5; it depends on their perception of risk. If the risk issues are low or it's a repeat purchase, they are unlikely to enter this phase. However, when risk issues are high because it's a large purchase, or the customer is new to buying this type of product/service, they will go through it.

What are the tell-tale signs of concerns that are not yet resolved? The obvious sign is things going quiet. The sale appears to be dead. Matters were progressing well, but now the customer won't say 'yes' for some reason.

Here are some dos and don'ts for handling this stage:

- **Do keep in touch** – Silence at this time is a real sin. It creates a communication vacuum, and that's something that selling abhors. If you're not filling the communication void, someone will – with concerns, competitors, fears and procrastination. Make an extra effort to talk to your contacts in the organisation. Find out what's happening. Ask questions like: 'How is everything going? What concerns do you have at this stage? How can I help?'
- **Do respect the customer's concerns** – The customer is like a friend about to undergo major surgery; your role is to help them through it. Show empathy and understanding. Be there to discuss any concerns they have. The relationship is everything.
- **Do explore the possibility of using 'like rank' selling** – Get your managing director to call their managing director. This is not a sales call, it's a relationship-building call. In his book *Selling to the Top*, David Peoples writes, 'Over the years I have made a study of lost accounts looking for common denominators to explain losses. They are hard to find . . . There is, however, one common denominator that appears with great consistency – the absence of an executive relationship.' Of course, the same applies when you are attempting to win the account in the first place.

- ■ **Don't make threats** – We've all done it. We're pulling our hair out thinking of ways to get a prevaricating customer to commit, and we think: 'I'll send an email saying we can only hold the quoted price until the 14th of the month' or some other 'gun to the head' idea. Don't do it! The customer knows you won't pull the trigger. You are damaging the long-term relationship on which everything ultimately depends. That all-important trust is becoming tainted. You are acting like a pushy salesperson, a description from which most of us would run a mile.

Once all their risk-related concerns are dealt with, the customer moves to Stage 6.

Stage 6 – Negotiate

Attention turns to improving the terms of the deal. The customer's concern is whether they can improve on the current proposal. They will either negotiate by themselves or wheel out the trained Rottweiler from their purchasing department.

Have you ever been involved in a sale where another person has joined the buying team towards the end? You haven't met this individual before, yet they seem to be a key player in tying up the details. The chances are that they are from the purchasing department. Their role is to improve the terms of the purchase so they can buy what they want, but at a better price.

The crucial area of negotiation warrants a chapter of its own and so will be discussed in detail in Chapter 8.

Once terms are agreed, the customer confirms the order and moves into the final stage of their buying process.

Stage 7 – Implementation

It is important for you to appreciate that it is only now that the sale *begins* for the customer. This is the time to really look after them and breathe life into their purchase. Their concerns are:

- ■ How well will it work?
- ■ How quickly will we get a return on our investment?
- ■ Will the supplier look after us?

Good implementation is an integral part of successful account management. If it goes well, you and your company are perceived as 'low risk'. The customer will be happy to provide you with references, giving you a powerful prospecting tool for future business.

> Several years ago, the Bristol and West Building Society was going through a major computer change. With 120 networked branches, each managing the account details of hundreds of customers, you can imagine the sensitivity of the implementation. On the Friday before the changeover, IBM's account manager called the CEO and said, 'It's a big weekend. I want you to be reassured that we're in control, everything is set fair, our people will be with your people all the time. Have a nice break and don't fret.'
>
> The following Monday, the account manager again spoke to the CEO. 'I know you will have already heard from your own people, but I just wanted to confirm that everything went according to plan. It's all bedding in nicely. I'm going to leave a couple of my guys with you until Wednesday to make sure.'
>
> The CEO was thrilled. He was hugely impressed by these calls and has been singing the praises of IBM ever since. The magic ingredient here is that IBM did not actually do anything more than it was contracted to do. Working over the weekend and leaving commissioning engineers on site until the Wednesday was all part of the sales agreement.
>
> The difference was that the account manager went out of his way to reassure the CEO, to keep him posted, to make him feel good about the changeover.
>
> There was also a software house involved in the same project. Their new applications worked fine, they were also on site all weekend and left technicians there until the Wednesday. However, they didn't take the time to reassure and communicate what they were doing. It was IBM's service that remained in the CEO's mind.

At every opportunity we should let customers know that we are looking after them. Let's get the credit for superb service, not in a pushy or egotistical way, but in a way that communicates that we have the customer's interests at heart.

▶ How the RACERNI® Process Helps

Once you really understand the RACERNI® buying process, you'll find that it helps in all sorts of ways. Here's how it benefited one of our clients, an established and respected IT reseller in the City.

> On being introduced to RACERNI®, the company realised that much of its new business was the result of enquiries coming in at the evaluation of options stage. This was either because manufacturers such as IBM, HP or Compaq had been the customer's first point of

contact, or another reseller had started the process, or the customer had initiated the project in isolation.

Although this company was brought in at that stage, it was successful in winning much of this business because it was able to differentiate itself strongly in areas such as technical expertise, testing facilities, and people at all levels who could relate to the customer's challenges. However, erosion of differentiators by other resellers posed the threat of a possible decline in its rate of growth in the future.

By changing its strategy and prospecting for new business projects in the 'recognition of gap' stage, it found that its salespeople could more easily influence the customer's criteria in favour of its key differentiators. Not only that, it was able to move outside its usual areas of success into more traditional industries where the potential for long-term growth was greater.

This strategy has been an outstanding success and the business continues to enjoy substantial growth.

▶ Psychology of the Buying Process Summary of Main Points

It is difficult to be an effective salesperson without a good insight into buying psychology, into why the customer buys. There are seven distinct psychological stages through which the buyer moves when making an important purchase. These are described by the acronym RACERNI®.

- **Recognise the gap.** The customer recognises a gap between what they are doing and what they could be doing.
- **Ask internally.** The customer asks, 'Is this gap large enough to justify action or are we happy to live with it?'
- **Criteria for ordering.** They draw up their initial specification.
- **Evaluate competing options.** They contact your competitors. Their concern is no longer 'Shall we buy?', but 'Who shall we buy from?'
- **Resolve their final concerns.** If it's a high-risk purchase, someone in the account steps in and raises a concern that causes the customer to become nervous.
- **Negotiate.** They turn their attention to improving the terms of the deal.
- **Implementation.** The sale begins for the customer. This is the time to really look after them. Good implementation is a must for successful account management.

4

Psychology of the Selling Process

Find out and match – the core of all selling and persuasion.

Chapter 3 considered the buying process – this chapter looks at the fundamental structure of selling and at the foundation on which all sales interactions are built. As any sports coach knows, you have to master the basics before you can compete at the top.

It is also important to appreciate that today *everyone* sells; not just outside the organisation but within it as well. The ability to persuade and influence is part of everyone's job. Whether we are selling, negotiating, marketing, advertising, coaching, leading, managing or speaking in public, we are persuading others to accept our ideas.

> Whatever your job description, you sell yourself everyday: your skills, your confidence, your personality, your warmth, your likeability, your competence.

Whether you're making a sales presentation, running for office, asking someone for a date, befriending a VIP, chairing a meeting, asking your boss for a promotion – whether you're a trainer, a manager, an author on a TV talk show, outcompeting everyone else for that job or out to make yourself a leader in your chosen field – whatever you're doing, the skills of persuasion are critical. We are always engaged in selling and it makes sense to have the clearest possible understanding of what the process is about. If we know exactly what we are aiming for, the words tend to take care of themselves.

If you've been in selling for a while, you'll be familiar with much of what you are about to read.

▶ The Art of Influence

The objective of all influence and all selling skills is to get the other person to act, to go ahead, to accept our idea. But how do we achieve this?

Action is the result of motivation. Consequently, any sales process should be motivational. However, be careful you don't confuse this with manipulation, which is hopelessly ineffective. To avoid misunderstanding, let's define them both:

- Motivation is getting people to do what *THEY* want.
- Manipulation is getting people to do what *WE* want.

No one is interested in what we want, they are interested in what they want. The two steps in a motivational, action-producing presentation therefore are:

- **Find out** what the customer wants.
- **Match** your product/service/idea to that.

That's it – that's the simple but potent key to successful selling. Selling can be described simply as helping people to get what they want. Can you recall the last time you made an important purchase, perhaps a car, a computer, a holiday or some new clothes? You had a requirement, and when you found what you wanted, you felt motivated to buy. Matching builds desire.

Find out and match is the fundamental psychology of persuasion. It always applies, whatever the situation:

- A speaker on the podium must know what the audience is interested in and match the presentation to that.
- Modern management thinking stresses the importance of matching the individual's personal goals to the goals of the organisation. How do you motivate an individual in your team? Find out what they want to achieve and match the task you have to that.
- The golden rule of coaching is 'they speak first'. In any people situation we should always begin by uncovering the other person's thoughts and concerns. Then it becomes clearer what input and guidance are required from us.
- When someone has a complaint, find out what they are unhappy about and ask, 'What would you like us to do about it?'

These examples all reinforce the concept of **find out and match**. To influence anyone, the core skill is: find out what's important to them, their hot button, and then match to it.

Not long ago I was returning to London from Glasgow on the shuttle and found myself sitting next to someone who turned out to be a very successful marketing communications consultant. The conversation inevitably came round to selling and I asked about her sales approach. Her answer was candid and succinct. 'I am simply interested in finding out what prospective clients are doing, explaining what I do and seeing if there is a fit.'

Find out and match is a strong reminder that questions, not reasons, form our main persuasive skill. In order to find out, we have to start by asking questions and listening carefully.

Good selling is a diagnostic process. This is one of the reasons why accountants and engineers can become skilled sellers. They are used to asking diagnostic questions.

▶ Four Steps in the Selling Process

If we add an opening and closing stage to the find out and match process, this provides us with a simple four-step sales structure:

1. Open
2. Find Out
3. Match
4. Close

To get a feel for the process, imagine you have a portable black box, roughly the size of a laptop, with four controls on it. At the beginning of every sale, you place this box in front of your customer and turn each control in sequence until you get the response, 'Yes, I'll have it.'

Obviously no actual black box exists, but it's helpful to regard the sales process as composed of four distinct control areas, each taking you one stage closer to winning the business.

Stage 1 – Open

This is the introduction to the sale. Imagine you meet a potential customer who doesn't know very much about your company and what you sell.

What is the first idea you have to sell to her? The answer is the idea that she wants to talk to you and is happy to answer your initial questions. The objective is to gain the customer's consent to move into a questioning phase.

This is achieved using an OHBS, an opening hot-button statement. This is a general, 'What's in it for her?' statement, designed to establish initial interest, rather like the opening sequence of an action movie.

Suppose you are selling accounting services. A typical OHBS would be: 'We've been able to assist a number of other organisations in a similar line to yourself in making substantial savings on their accounting costs. At this stage I have no idea what you consider to be important in this area, so would it be OK if I were to ask you a few straightforward questions so I understand more about your business and your requirement?'

Work out your own OHBS using this approach. Don't oversell and keep it short. Obviously you should only make statements you can justify.

If your customer has already expressed interest – perhaps she answered an ad, or a direct mailshot, or simply called us as a result of a recommendation. Then the OHBS is probably not required.

The higher the customer's initial interest, the less important the opening statement is. That said, it's always a good idea to warm the customer up with a statement about what's in it for her.

Recently I was in the sales office of a new property development in southern Spain. The first thing the salesperson asked me was, 'Have you been here before? What size of house are you interested in? What price range are you looking at? Do you have an existing property to sell?' This really annoyed me. I know salespeople are taught to ask questions, but I sensed I was being qualified and I didn't like it.

What went wrong here? The salesperson made two errors. First, he launched into his questions too eagerly without warming up my interest. Secondly, it was all too obvious that the questions were serving his agenda, not mine. This was information he needed to know in order to make a sale. That's why he turned me off.

What should he do in future? Well, he might like to begin with an OHBS to create initial interest. For example, he could briefly explain why the location is good and why the builder is credible. Then seek the customer's consent to ask some questions: 'Would it be OK if I ask you one or two straightforward questions about your requirements?' And finally, and most significantly, he must make sure that the questions find out what is important to the customer, not him. That's the critical area.

How rumours affect the sale

In every sale we must find out what the customer has heard about our company before we begin. Once a product or service becomes established in a market, opinions pass around about it and what it does or does not do. And rumours and opinions can now spread particularly quickly via email, bulletin boards and Internet chat rooms. As Amazon chief executive Jeff Bezos comments, 'Word of mouth is incredibly powerful online. A dissatisfied customer can tell 1,000 people in a few minutes.'

If the customer has heard a positive rumour, something good about your product or company, naturally you want to know about this. It helps to boost your confidence and enthusiasm.

Similarly, if the customer has heard a negative rumour, this is a mismatch clattering around in the back of her mind that must be handled at the beginning of the sale, otherwise it will almost certainly cause difficulties towards the end.

Either way, you must find out what she knows about you. Ask such questions as:

- 'What do you know about us?'
- 'Do you know any companies using our web design service?'
- 'What do you know about our optic fibre repeaters?'

If the customer replies, 'We used you two years ago and felt your support and service left a lot to be desired', you must address that concern immediately.

Be up front. 'Yes, we did get it wrong, however since then we have redesigned the way we operate and turned that area into a strength, and that's what I'd like to discuss with you. Here's what some of our customers are saying about us now . . .'

Stage 2 – Find Out

Once you have gained the customer's consent to ask her some questions, you can find out information that enables you to understand her requirement. Use questions such as:

- 'What are you looking for?'
- 'What factors are important to you?'
- 'What do you want to achieve?'
- 'What would a company have to offer for you to do business with it?'
- 'Where could your present system be improved?'
- 'What criteria would you use in choosing a supplier?'

When the customer responds, listen intensely. Really hearing everything someone says to you is one of the real skills of selling.

Note that here we are assuming that the customer does have a requirement. If she doesn't or says she's happy with her current arrangements, then you need to use the gap analysis techniques outlined in Chapter 7.

Shape, guide and modify

Imagine you are in the process of finding out what is wanted and the customer brings up a requirement that you cannot match. What do you do?

You shape, guide and modify it with her agreement into one that you can match. It's important to appreciate that buyers expect their requirements to be shaped by coming into contact with the marketplace. This happens in most sales and customers welcome it.

For example, I recently purchased a new video camera. Not knowing much about what was currently available, I talked to various suppliers who shaped and guided my ideas about the best solution for my requirements. I both expected and welcomed this process because it helped me to clarify what I wanted.

It goes without saying that if there is absolutely no way any kind of match is conceivable, then any amount of shaping, guiding and modifying won't work. A customer is never going to buy something she doesn't want. But if the solution is almost there, then this is a perfectly acceptable part of the consultative process.

> One of my colleagues tells the story of buying his first flat in London many years ago. After deciding that renting was no longer for him, he drew up a list of criteria for the flat: where it should be located; number of bedrooms; number of bathrooms; what floor it should be on; size of reception rooms; price bracket, and so on. He contacted a number of estate agents and eventually purchased a property.
> Do you suppose this was an exact match to his original criteria? No – it wasn't even in the same area. His requirements had been shaped, guided and modified by coming into contact with the marketplace. But he didn't walk into his new flat thinking, 'They shaped, guided and modified me.' He was delighted with it, an entirely satisfied customer.

Stage 3 – Match

When we have established the requirement we move to the sales presentation itself. This stage has one function and one function only, to show the customer how the proposed solution **matches** their requirement.

This is where we show our enthusiasm, passion and belief in what we offer. The best way to be convincing is to be convinced. Passion persuades.

To strut our stuff effectively, we have to believe that our proposed solution is absolutely right for the customer. The first sale we have to make each day is to ourselves.

One trap that salespeople fall into here is adding more features and benefits than are required. This is a hangover from traditional sales training that taught you to learn all the features of your product (what it *is*) and their corresponding benefits (what it *does*), package them together and that's your presentation.

That's not the way to do it. The correct approach is to sell matching benefits. What makes product A superior to product B is not the fact that it has more benefits, but that it does more of what the customer wants it to do, i.e. it has more matching benefits.

Only talk about those features and benefits that match the customer's requirement. If a product has 10 component features but during the **find out** stage it becomes clear that only three are important, then these three are the ones the salesperson describes during the **matching** stage. Adding more information than required simply blunts the accuracy of the sales process.

> Think about an analogy with a sharp pencil. If you turn it upside down and push the blunt top against your hand, it doesn't hurt. However, if you take the sharp end and do the same, it hurts a great deal. The blunt end represents *all* the features and benefits of your product/service – the unwanted ones prevent the others from penetrating. The sharp end represents the matching benefits – the components that count for this customer. Including these and only these ensures that your presentation is accurate and clear.

Stage 4 – The Close

Once the matching stage is complete, you can move to the close.

Closing is straightforward. There is no mystique, nothing magical – you close business by asking for it. Customers expect a good salesperson to ask for the order at the end of a presentation, so don't disappoint them.

If you dither at the close, you affect everything that has happened previously. The world belongs to the askers.

Whenever salespeople discuss the topic of closing, the question invariably crops up: When should you close? Is there a perfect psychological moment to ask for the business?

Viewed through the lens of our core skill, **find out and match,** the answer is obvious: you ask for the business whenever the matching is complete.

This may take two hours, two months, two years or two minutes depending on the size and complexity of the sale, how well your company is known, risk issues and a hundred other factors.

Don't close too early

What happens if you ask for the business before the matching is complete, before the customer can see how your solution satisfactorily meets their requirements? The customer says no, usually with a courteous 'I want to think about it' or some other objection. It is important to appreciate that traditional 'objections' are more accurately described as 'areas of mismatch'. The customer is not yet convinced that your solution is the right one for her.

To avoid asking for the business too early, before closing we must find out whether we have achieved a good match or whether we still have more work to do.

Sometimes this is obvious from the customer's comments. However, if you are unsure, test the matching by asking a test close question. Here are four examples:

- 'How do you feel about it?'
- 'How does that strike you?'
- 'Do you have a date in mind?'
- 'Are you happy with everything we've discussed so far?'

If you get a positive response – 'Yes, it looks good' – you have a green light to move on to the final close and ask for the order – 'Would you like to go ahead?'

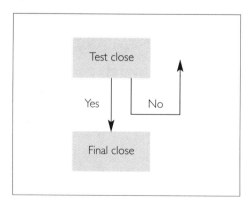

If you get a negative response, hold off. It means that there are still some mismatches or unanswered concerns in the customer's mind and there is no point in closing at this time. Instead, loop back and find out what she is unsure about, deal with it and close again. The LACPAAC® model discussed in Appendix II takes you through this process.

Final closing questions

Asking for the business should feel comfortable and easy. If it doesn't, the chances are you are asking too soon.

Of course it's a tense moment – you may have been working on this sale for months. Perhaps the bonus attached to it makes the difference to your getting a bigger mortgage on a property you want or finally getting that new kitchen you've set your heart on. The important thing is not to let that show. If the customer picks up any nervousness it could give them cause for cold feet.

Practise closing and sounding natural. Don't be too confident, but do be keen, friendly and self-assured. Find a way of asking for the business that is and sounds comfortable for you.

Here are three approaches. Keep in mind that it's not important how you ask, as long as you do. As Mae West once remarked, 'He who hesitates is a damned fool.'

The next steps close

One of the simplest techniques is to talk about next steps. When you believe the customer is ready to buy, start discussing implementation details:

- 'What dates do you have in mind for this project?'
- 'Who shall I coordinate with in your office?'
- 'Who should our technical people speak to regarding installation of the new software?'
- 'Who would you like to send on the January course?'

Once the customer joins you in discussing these details, the sale is effectively closed.

The direct close

This is a straightforward request for the business. It is uncomplicated and reflects the salesperson's confidence in the solution. As always, it must only be used when you know you have a satisfactory match.

- 'So there you are . . . Would you like to go ahead?'

This is one of my favourite closes. It's worked for me time after time in every industry in which I've been involved. There is no mystique – it's clear, to the point, and everyone knows what the expected outcome is.

Another favourite is:

- 'How would you like to go forward?'

This is soft, easy to say and always sounds appropriate – perfect for consultative-partner selling.

Here are some other examples. Pick the ones you feel comfortable with and use your words, not mine.

- 'Shall I put you down for 10 terminals?'
- 'Can I have your OK to start delivery next week?'
- 'Can we install it for you right away?'
- 'Can we call it a deal?'
- 'How about it, can we go ahead right away?'
- 'Will you give us your approval to go ahead?'
- 'Can we have your order?'

The alternative close

This is a popular form of closing question for simple sales. We give the customer a choice between two alternatives: a choice of delivery date, financial arrangements, quantity, colour etc. The choice should be of a minor nature and both alternatives should be attractive to the customer. Her answer reflects her personal preference. When she answers she has committed herself to order.

- 'Would you like delivery this month or next?'
- 'Would you prefer to invest in this outright or make use of our leasing arrangements?'
- 'This projector comes in two colours, blue and grey. They are both popular, which one would you prefer?'
- 'Do you want to handle this by credit card or cheque?'

> My wife Catherine and I have three terrific children, but they are still very young and getting them to go to bed at a sensible time can be somewhat fraught. So we've learned to say to them, 'Do you want to go to bed at 8.00 or 8.30?' Naturally they always pick 8.30, but at that time off they go. So far it's working well!

The important aspect of closing, as the Nike strapline puts it, is: 'Just Do It'.

The power of silence

After you ask for the business, keep quiet and wait for the other person to respond. It is natural for people to hesitate just before they buy.

If you have difficulty with this, here's a tip – after asking the question, count slowly to yourself 1, 2, 3, 4 . . . This helps you keep your cool.

But if the silence continues too long for comfort, then you must interrupt. Here's a great way of handling the situation. After a significant time has elapsed and you feel you have to speak, smile (everything is soluble in a smile) and quietly and respectfully say, 'Someone once told me that silence means consent, was he right?' You have interrupted the silence by asking the customer another closing question. That's businesslike and professional. In most cases the customer will say 'yes'. She may even laugh and you have the business.

Are closing techniques still relevant?

Some people say that in the era of consultative-partner selling, closing is no longer necessary. An article recently published in a management journal quoted a trainer who wrote, 'Forget about those closing techniques.' The impression is given that closing belongs to yesterday's sales skills and that if you have an excellent relationship and match the customer's requirements, the sale will take care of itself.

That's just not true. Such thinking may elicit cheers from the uninvolved, but it doesn't stand up to any reality check.

Yesterday's sales skills certainly put way too much emphasis on the role of closing – phrases such as 'close early and often' and 'always be closing' are clearly nonsense – but you still have to ask for the business, otherwise the other party may simply procrastinate.

At the end of a presentation, after all your hard work, the pot is boiling hot and interest is high. That's the time to ask for the business or gain commitment to take it to the next stage, otherwise your customer's interest gradually cools until it eventually goes cold.

> I recall, as a prospective customer, sitting in a boardroom discussing the purchase of a freehold office building in which my company was interested. At one stage in the meeting I felt myself beginning to procrastinate, to back off; not for any particular reason, it was just a big decision.
>
> The manager of the property development company that owned the building smiled and said, 'We are here today to reach agreement so this transaction can take place. Are you happy to do that?'
>
> I agreed and we did the deal that morning. It was an excellent buy. He helped me to make up my mind and get things moving.

Most customers need help in making up their mind – that's the role of closing. Having said that, you will, I'm sure, have experienced a situation where you have made such an excellent presentation that the customer is completely convinced and is so eager to get the ball rolling that she says, 'OK, I'm happy, where do I sign?' before you get the chance to ask. This is fantastic when it happens – but don't rely on it!

Which quadrant are you in?

How 'closing' or 'gaining commitment' skills fit with relationship selling is best described by the following matrix.

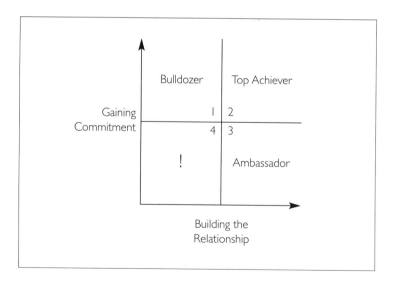

Let's look at the characteristics of each quadrant:

Quadrant 1: The Bulldozer. Here we have the old-style sellers. They are great at gaining commitment, but lousy at building relationships. They know every close in the book. They bulldoze their way to some success, but find it increasingly tough in front of the new customer who wants a relationship with their supplier. They are the dinosaurs of selling.

Quadrant 2: Top Achiever. Here we have those who are *both* excellent relationship builders and skilled at gaining commitment. This combination perfectly describes the consultative-partner selling style and is the quadrant to aim for.

Quadrant 3: The Ambassador. Here we have those who are great at building relationships, but not effective at gaining commitment. Everyone likes them and comes to them for advice – but often end up buying elsewhere.

An investment banker told me recently how her people had become very skilled at networking within customer accounts. They were 'covering the bases' and 'mapping' their accounts superbly.

But they were not getting any more business and she was concerned.

This is a typical example of how relationship building by itself is not enough. It must be coupled with the skills of gaining commitment, otherwise the sale doesn't move forward.

To help with this, it's a great idea before any sales call to ask yourself, 'What do I want to happen as a result of this call?' That's what you close the meeting on.

Quadrant 4: Inhabitants of this quadrant are poor at both building relationships and gaining commitment. They are usually unemployed or about to be. Disrespectful colleagues refer to them as *pond life*! This may sound a little rude, but I'm sure you have your own name for people in this quadrant that may be even less complimentary!

Closing the group presentation

Most of us encounter the beauty parade scenario where several suppliers are lined up to present their proposals to the buying team.

Opportunities exist to close here as well.

How often have we finished our presentation, after hours of preparation, thanked our audience and started to pack up? I know you wouldn't do this, but you'd be amazed how many otherwise highly skilled sellers do.

Why not say:

'Can I take this opportunity to ask you how closely you feel we've met your brief this afternoon?'

or:

'How comfortable are you with what we've presented today?'

or:

'How would you like to go forward?'

▶ Psychology of the Selling Process Summary of Main Points

The fundamental structure of selling is **find out and match**. Selling can be defined as helping people to get what they want.

This can be expanded to a four-step sales process:

- **Open**. Begin the sale with a general 'what's in it for the customer' statement to warm things up and gain consent to move into a questioning phase. Establish trust and build rapport.
- **Find out**. Ask probing questions to understand the customer's requirement. Shape, guide and modify as necessary.
- **Match**. Provide the appropriate solution. Show the customer how your proposed solution matches their requirement. Only talk about those features and benefits that match. Be accurate.
- **Close**. When you know the matching is complete, ask for the business: Would you like to go ahead? How would you like to go forward?

Part Three
SELLING SKILLS

5
Finding New Business

Powerful prospecting tips for initiating sales.

Let's now switch gears. Parts I and II considered the selling concept and the processes underlying buying and selling. This part of the book takes a step back and focuses on the skills that you as a salesperson need in your day-to-day interactions with customers.

We start with identifying new sources of business. This is often not an easy task. 'Put me in front of a prospective client and I'm pretty good,' says John, a business development manager for a communications consultancy. 'The hard bit is getting there.'

Most people who say they really enjoy prospecting probably lie about other things as well. On a list of activities sellers feel good about, it usually lies somewhere between public speaking and bungee jumping. Nevertheless, finding a source of new customers is where selling begins.

Unless you get good at getting in front of new customers, be it face to face or on the telephone, all your other skills count for nothing. This chapter is about making it a strength, not an Achilles' heel, by concentrating on six important habits.

▶ I – Be disciplined

This is common sense, but it's not always common practice. Make an appointment with yourself to do prospecting for one hour each day. Finding new customers is the number one priority when it comes to planning your time.

The secret is to do it continuously, otherwise you follow a feast or famine cycle when you oscillate between good and bad months. If you haven't been prospecting for a while, you can't suddenly conjure up new sales. If it takes your customers four to eight weeks to decide to go ahead, you have to wait that long to get numbers on the board again.

Make as many calls as possible in your prospecting hour and don't get phased by those who have no interest. Have the attitude that people either do want to hear what you have to offer or they don't. If you get a 'no', simply go on to the next call. Monitor your hit rate – if you get one appointment or one sale for every six calls, then each 'no' simply takes you one step closer to a 'yes'.

As high wire artist Karl Wallenda says, 'Being on the tightrope is living, everything else is just waiting.'

▶ 2 – Overcome Reluctance

I remember how hard it was to make those initial calls early in my career. I used to sit there staring at the phone. I'd pick it up and think, 'No way, I can't call. He won't want to speak to me. I'll feel an idiot.' So I'd put the phone down again.

Most salespeople have been in that position. The solution is to think about the value you offer the customer. Once you realise that the customer gets the most benefit from the transaction, you get enthused and your reluctance to call disappears. Imagine that your customer desperately needs your product or service. He is hoping that you'll call, even if he seems reluctant at first. Your mindset needs to be that you've got good news.

The most successful financial services salesperson of all time was Ben Feldman. During the 1970s Ben personally outsold 1,500 of the industry's top 1,800 *companies* each year. When prospecting for business, he knew the importance of a positive mindset. Before a call he told himself, 'This client is desperately underinsured. Thank goodness I've called.'

Follow Ben's advice. Before you pick up the phone, visualise the customer eagerly awaiting your call. After you introduce yourself, picture the customer responding, 'Where have you been? I need to talk to you.'

And remember, the most efficient use of cold calling time is to follow up prospective customers you have already written to or contacted.

Recall past success

If a new salesperson came up to you and asked when the very best time is to make a sale, how would you reply?

The answer, of course, is just after you've made one. After a sale we're on a high, we're on a roll, we're in a selling mode. We can't wait to get out there and do it again. We are energised because of our achievement. So before any sales call, pause and think of the last time you sold well. Think of a prospecting activity that went well. Replay it in your mind's eye.

Whatever we think about grows stronger. The salesperson who before a call remembers a previous time when it didn't go well is setting himself up for more of the same. Recalling past success is an excellent way of enhancing your self-confidence and beating the fear of rejection. I love those T-shirts that proclaim 'No Fear'.

Be disciplined with your thought processes as well as your time.

▶ 3 – Be a master of follow-up

My first sales manager told me that the person who masters follow-up, masters selling. Just like a golf or tennis shot, the power is in the follow-through.

Maintain a dialogue with those leads and those clients you are currently working with. The golden rule is to keep in touch.

I've lost count of the salespeople who call our office to interest us in their product or service once or maybe twice and then never call us again. Keep plugging away with meticulous courtesy and I promise you will make more sales. Persistence is persuasive. As we saw in Chapter 1, people want to do business with those who really want it. You never lose a sale until you decide to quit.

Your next call, even if it's the seventh one to the same person in the last six months, could be the one that opens up the business. Just because a customer doesn't have a current requirement doesn't mean they won't next year or the year after. Keep in touch.

If the customer tells you to call back in two years and one month's time because that's when the contract with their existing supplier expires, do it. Nothing should be allowed to slip through the cracks.

Ever wonder why Coke and Pepsi run ads throughout the year? Surely everyone knows about them, so why continue to advertise? Big advertisers have learned that knowing about a brand isn't enough; the decision to buy is also influenced by how recently we heard about it.

What does this mean for you? It's not simply how long you've been calling a customer or how many times you have spoken to them that counts – it's how close your last contact was to the time when they are ready to buy.

You need to establish a *regular contact schedule* with every key customer. Visit in person, use the telephone and, in between, send a letter, brochure, article reprint or something else that will keep your name in the forefront of the customer's mind at least once a month.

We're happy with our existing supplier

Keep in mind that all relationships ebb and flow, they have good times and not so good times. If your customers say they are happy with their current supplier, the soundest policy is to be patient, and to be tastefully persistent by keeping your name in front of the customer. Write to them, send them relevant testimonials, call them every two or three months – build a relationship (there are some suggestions for how to do this in Chapter 6). Solidly position yourself as number 2. Their existing supplier may become complacent or the salesperson may leave. You will then be well positioned to win the business. If you position yourself as number 2 in enough companies, sooner or later you are going to be number 1 in some of them.

Never fall into the trap of assuming that your customers are only interested in your company and your product. Instead, take it for granted that they are being bombarded, induced and seduced by all sorts of other products, services and suppliers.

Proposals and quotations

Have you ever been in this situation when, after a meeting or two, the customer asks you to put things in writing by giving them a proposal?

You present the proposal and the customer explains their time-frame for making a decision. But nothing happens. What do you do? The sale is gradually slipping away. You know that if you call the customer yet again to ask how the decision is going, that's being a pest. So how do you keep the sale alive after you have delivered the proposal?

The secret is to *hold something back*. Don't put all the information in the original proposal. Then when you feel the sale dragging, drop a customer testimonial letter or article reprint in the post with a covering note: 'I thought you might find this letter from one of our clients interesting and I look forward to achieving similar results for you.'

▶ 4 – Explore different approaches

Using the telephone to call up prospective customers and sell the appointment not the product or service is the classic approach to finding new customers. However, the marketplace is changing thanks to the information revolution.

Today's customers have better knowledge, more choices and an increasing variety of ways of conducting business with suppliers. Some prefer to deal face to face; some prefer to deal on the telephone; some prefer to deal on the net with 24-hour call centre support.

As always, you must adjust your method of selling to suit the customer. Some may prefer never to see you, others may insist you visit. How do *your* customers prefer to buy?

Most of us think our larger accounts require face-to-face selling and telesales or resellers can look after the smaller fish. Maybe that's right, maybe not – it depends on the customer. Nothing is more infuriating than a salesperson who insists that all discussions require a face-to-face meeting – they don't.

With all the information available to them, customers know much more than they used to about the benefits of your products and services. I believe this makes it easier to sell to them. They are either in the market for your product or they're not. This means you can use the first telephone contact to advance the sale further than before, which saves wasting time and expense on fruitless appointments. If a customer is not ready, willing and able to buy, there's very little you can do to change the situation, so you might as well find this out on the telephone.

Personally I have always found it more effective to ask some initial probing questions during a cold call and not just go straight for the appointment. Let me stress that you must be the judge as to what will work best in your business environment.

A suggested lead in for the initial telephone contact is discussed in Appendix I.

Here's a selection of useful questions. Pick the ones that suit you and use your words not mine:

- 'Can I ask you what you're doing now about XYZ?'
- 'Is it meeting your requirements or do you feel there is room for improvement?'
- 'If you had a free hand to make any improvement you wanted, what would it be?'

- 'Are there any circumstances in which you would consider a change?'
- 'What do you want to achieve in the next 12 months?'
- 'How are you going to get to where you want to be?'
- 'What criteria would you use to choose the right supplier for you?'
- 'What would you need from us to decide whether you would like to work with us?'
- 'Is there anyone else in the organisation you'd like to bring in to help you evaluate what we do?'

You may notice these questions offer a variety of different styles – open, closed and alternative.

In the real world we shouldn't set ourselves to one style only. The secret of good questioning is to probe areas that hook the customer's interest – whatever that style may be.

To achieve unusual results, we must sometimes use unusual methods.

- Stockbroker Stephen Anderson pulled in hundreds of thousands in cold call commissions with an innovative approach. To distinguish himself from the pack, he developed an audio business card. These worked so well that colleagues and clients began asking for the cards to market their own services. His customers range from stockbrokers to plastic surgeons. Each audio card carries a message from the salesperson, a question and answer session and, on side B, testimonials from top clients. It's so distinctive that even customers drowning in junk mail will give it a listen. The way you're received when you call back after the customer has heard your tape is far better than how they normally take your calls.
- Recently I met a CEO who had purchased a new BMW over the Internet. He had completed an online questionnaire and within 48 hours had been called by one of Autobytel's dealers with a no-haggle, low price made possible by the low cost of the Internet-originated transaction. The dealer had explained the purchase cost and the markup involved. 'Wouldn't you prefer to deal face to face?' I asked him. 'No,' he replied, 'this was easier, cheaper and quicker.'

■ One survey conducted by a computer manufacturer asked what channels people would be willing to use to buy a mainframe computer: 21 per cent of respondents said they would be willing to buy over the phone. Four per cent – that's one in 25 – said they would buy over the Internet. People are much more willing to buy through low-cost channels than many of us believe.

Handling Voicemail

I get many requests on how to handle voicemail. Love it or hate it, voicemail is part of the new business scene.

Be positive about it rather than frustrated by it. You have an opportunity to leave an advertising message you know the customer will listen to. You can make your point without interruption. And you can still ask one or two questions to get the customer thinking.

Here are some guidelines:

1. Be enthusiastic and personable. Your message must stand out from the rest when played back.
2. Use an opening hot button statement to raise interest.
3. Ask one or two questions. Questions not reasons are your main persuasive skills.
4. Introduce a USP. Again rotate it into a question.
5. Keep it brief.
6. Follow up with a letter or email enclosing testimonials or article reprints.
7. Leave another message the following month with your second USP.
8. Leave another message the following month with your third USP.

Here's an example:

'Hello. This is Robin Fielder from Leadership Development. We're a sales and management training company and we have a new approach to sales training based on the consultative-partner selling style. I was calling to ask you what you were doing about introducing new sales skills to your team and what importance you attach to personal development training, so your people have both the skill to win and the will to win. At this stage I have no idea whether this would be appropriate for you. If you would like to discuss it, please call me on 020 7381 6233.'

▶ 5 – Ask for Referrals

Something that never ceases to amaze me is the effort that many organisations direct towards getting new business while overlooking their existing client base. That's crazy – it's like filling a bucket that has a hole in it.

Your best prospects are your existing customers. There is an incredibly effective technique for tapping this resource, a technique that provides real insight into how you get qualified leads. Are you ready for it? **Ask** for them!

Asking for referrals works, but you have to *do* it. You have to ask: 'Who else in the organisation do you feel could benefit from our services?'

Most customers understand the need to sell, but be careful. Whatever you do, don't say, 'By the way John, could you give me some names of other people we should contact?' The answer will be, '*By the way*, no.' 'By the way' implies this is not important.

Here's how to do it. Choose an appropriate moment, ideally when you know the customer is satisfied or, better, delighted with what your organisation has achieved, and say: 'We're on a new business drive and I have been asked to produce two new introductions this month. Can you help?'

Now add one of the most effective referral questions ever devised: 'If you and I swapped jobs tomorrow, who would be the first person you would call? Would you mind if I contacted them? May I use your name?'

This approach has worked for me in every business in which I've been involved. However, be careful you don't take its power away by asking for three or four names. That's too difficult. Ask your customers for *one* name and help them to focus. If they want to give you two or three names, they'll tell you anyway.

▶ 6 – Use a Database Prospecting System

Once all the obvious sources of leads have been exhausted, most of us think about buying in lists. But what do we do with them?

Direct mail is hit and miss. If it ever worked it was for small order values and response rates were generally around 2 per cent. Most direct mail goes in the bin and very few cold calls result in sales opportunities, because customers are reluctant to buy from people they don't know or trust.

The solution is to apply the principles of consultative-partner selling to lead generation. But how do you establish a relationship with a customer you haven't yet met?

The system you are about to learn was taught to me by David Marsh, a valued client and marketing director for a multinational insurance brokerage. David used a similar system all over the world and averaged a 10 per cent closing rate from cold. This is a highly professional, soft-sell approach that you can use in any business to warm up the customer and get your message across.

It does take time and thought to set up, but the returns are out of all proportion to the effort required. There are four steps involved.

Step 1 – Find the names

Each salesperson can handle about 300 prospects, but to start with obtain, say, 600 names, addresses and telephone numbers in your target market for each member of the team. You can purchase these from such companies as Dun & Bradstreet, Jordans or Greens. You can also buy CD-ROMs with enormous amounts of information about every conceivable type of business. You need to specify industries not required, if any; turnover level, e.g. £5m to £50m; and geographical area.

Your targeting must be personalised, so make sure before you buy that the list will contain the names of the people to whom you want to write. You may need to target more than one person.

This discussion obviously refers to business-to-business selling, but you can use the system for any target market. If you can acquire names and addresses, you can use this system.

Step 2 – Telephone to check names

This can be done by a temporary secretary who calls to confirm the name of, say, the finance director, his full title and address. This is also the time to delete competitors, businesses closed, decisions made elsewhere and any existing customers who appear on the list. Typically by now the list will have been reduced to 300.

These qualifying calls can be completed in about two weeks. The checked database is held on a PC that will address the personalised letters and envelopes automatically.

Step 3 – Write to each prospective customer once a month for at least three months

Steps 1 and 2 are nothing new. Step 3 is the juice of the system. This is how you initiate the relationship.

You write once a month for three months, enclosing a one-page newsletter. The object is not to sell but to *begin the relationship*. You are friendly, not 'pushy'. The only person the customer feels comfortable talking with about their requirements is a friend first and a salesperson second.

The newsletter should contain relevant information for any potential purchaser in your market sector. Typically it should have three or four paragraphs of, say, five lines each. Include product application examples, changes in the market, new concepts, management ideas and, if appropriate, rate/price trends. Tailor it to suit your business.

The objective is for your customer to think that you know their business.

What information would your potential customers be interested in? Brainstorm the material you will include. You can do this for yourself, or get together with your colleagues. If you are fortunate enough to have one, speak to your marketing/PR department.

There is no push whatsoever for an appointment in these newsletters. You are merely establishing your credentials, your professionalism and your willingness to help the customer. Everyone wants to deal with the person with the best knowledge.

This is the sequence:

- Month 1: Send 300 letters with an attached newsletter and company brochure or other 'credentials' document. Your covering letter should introduce the newsletter.
- Month 2: Send 300 letters with a second newsletter, together with a product sheet or relevant article. Invite the customer to let you know if there is anything they would like to see in the newsletter.
- Month 3: Send 300 letters with a third newsletter.

By writing each month for three months, you are building the relationship. That's why it works.

After each person on the list has received three newsletters, move to Step 4.

Step 4 – Telephone to ask about the newsletter and make the appointment

Ask whether the customer likes the newsletter. How can we improve it? What would you like to see in the next edition?

If you establish rapport, ask about the customer's business. When it feels like the right time, ask for the appointment.

If the customer seems frosty or disinterested, ask, 'Would you mind if I left you on the mailing list for six months?'

The customer will probably say 'yes' just to get rid of you. But may also be thinking, 'He's a persistent so-and-so. I wish our sales-people were more like that.'

Then call again in three months. Ultimately, of course, you must decide how many months you are going to persist with a particular customer.

▶ Finding New Business Summary of Main Points

Prospecting is where selling begins. Here are six ideas that set the scene:

- **Be disciplined**. Make an appointment with yourself for a minimum of one hour each day for prospecting.
- **Overcome reluctance**. Once you realise that the customer benefits most from the transaction, reluctance to call disappears. Enthusiasm is a much better way than rational argument for overcoming resistance.
- **Be a master of follow-up**. Keep plugging away with meticulous courtesy and you'll make more sales. Maintain regular contact. Have something new to say on each occasion.
- **Explore different approaches**. To achieve unusual results we must sometimes use unusual methods.
- **Ask for referrals**. If you and I swapped jobs tomorrow, who would be the first person you would call?
- **Use a database prospecting system**. To initiate the relationship, write to potential customers once a month for three months, enclosing a newsletter. Then telephone.

6

Building the Relationship

Be a partner – the magic ingredient for getting all the business, not just one transaction.

We discussed in Part I and Chapter 5 the importance of relationships in twenty-first-century selling. Your competitors will copy your product-based USPs at every opportunity, but the one ingredient they can't replicate is the relationship you have with your customer. Nurture it at every opportunity. Rather than just asking yourself 'How can I win this business by the end of the day, week, month?', ask yourself, 'What could this relationship look like in 12 months? Or two years? Or five years?'

This is the *partner* element of consultative-partner selling. And whether you sell software, financial services, consulting or whatever, it's where the action is.

The software salesperson says, 'I'm not here to sell you the latest application. I'm here to be your software consultant for as long as you are using computers. We're in this together.'

The financial services salesperson says, 'I'm not here to sell you a policy. I'm here to be your long-term financial adviser.'

Faced with decreasing product differences, the relationship is your principal source of competitive advantage. People will even buy an inferior product from a superior relationship.

> Customers are not buying product leadership. They are buying a trusted consultant.

Good relationships promote customer loyalty and high repeat business. That usually means higher profits.

According to a recent survey by consultants Bain & Company, Leo Burnett, one of the largest advertising agencies in the world, has a near-perfect 98 per cent customer retention rate. The agency has grown to 63 offices worldwide without ever raising capital by issuing shares or borrowing heavily. Leo Burnett staff are among the highest paid in the industry and their prices are among the most competitive. That's the tangible value of relationship building.

But what about companies that attract new customers with price discounts and special offers? Is that a good idea? It works, but a customer easily hooked by a minimal price will just as easily abandon you at the next discount offered by your competitor.

If that's how your firm attracts new business, focus hard on building a personal relationship with each new customer. That way they'll stay.

▶ Trust

Trust is the key to building relationships. It's the glue that holds them together. Modern selling is based on the ability to establish trust.

To become a successful salesperson you must shift from selling products and services to selling not only solutions, but *confidence and dependability*. You must be totally reliable to deal with in every respect. The phrase 'a trusted consultant' describes it well.

Resistance comes from mistrust. When a customer won't share their real requirements with you, there's not much you can do. The way to overcome that is to build up so much trust and confidence that the customer will instinctively tell you everything you need to know.

▶ How to Establish Trust

If you want to send a powerful message of trust to your customers and those around you, follow the principles described below.

Be other person centred

Once people sense you have *their* interests at heart, not just your own, they begin to trust you.

This fits well with the concept of selling solutions. Develop a passionate interest in helping others to achieve their objectives. Have a tireless curiosity about the customer's world. What you hand out you get back, usually multiplied.

To get into the top 10 per cent of salespeople, you must be involved not only in the success of your business, but in the success of your customer's business. When you help a customer win, that customer in turn helps you to win. You have a *partnership*.

> I well remember dealing with a young and exceptionally keen
> audiovisual consultant who went so far as to insist I had his home
> number in case we had any difficulties during out-of-work hours. I
> never did call, but appreciated the gesture. It said, 'I'm here to support
> you and have real confidence in my product.'

Being other person centred also means being flexible. A willingness
to adjust our viewpoint to incorporate other people's ideas is one
of the key skills of persuasion. Mostly this goes without saying when
we are with customers, but what about when we are with internal
colleagues?

As we saw in Chapter 1, team selling is increasingly the way
forward. Once colleagues realise that we are flexible enough to listen
to their views and respond to their concerns, they are much more
likely to buy into our proposals.

Do what is best for the customer

You should be as reliable as the customer's own staff in making
recommendations. In every situation, do the best for the customer
regardless. Be bias free.

This also means that if your solution is not the right one, tell them
and recommend what they should do. Maybe you'll lose some
business, but the customer won't forget your integrity.

> We have used the same firm of litho printers for many years. I recall
> asking for a quote on a large print run for looseleaf inserts and the
> owner manager, Ernie Collins, saying, 'It would probably be cheaper for
> you to print this job on a web machine. We don't have one but can put
> you in touch with a reliable firm.'
> I knew he was turning down a potentially lucrative order to give us his
> best advice. It significantly reinforced the feeling of trust and reassured
> us that our print supplier was the right one, even if we could get the
> printing done cheaper elsewhere.

Before any sales managers throw their hands up in horror, we are
not talking about recommending a direct competitor – we are
talking about doing the best for your customer in non-competing
areas.

Listen

The more you listen, the more you are fascinated by what people
have to say, the more they will like you, trust you and want to do
business with you.

When the *customer* speaks, the skilled salesperson listens with full attention. When you listen, you learn what matters to the customer. And there's an added bonus – listeners quickly become popular.

Below-average people monopolise the talking. Above-average people monopolise the listening.

> Martina King, Managing Director of Capital Radio in London, tells the story of how she called on a prospective customer and somehow allowed the prospect to tell her about his family, his kids and all the difficulties he was encountering. Driving back after the meeting, Martina thought what a waste of time that was. She felt guilty at not making her presentation and selling her product.
>
> The next day he phoned and booked an ad – the first ever from that account.

Rapt attention is the highest form of flattery. Listen to people as if you have all the time in the world. Whenever you speak to a customer, visualise a neon sign above their head reading *'Make me feel important'*. That is just as vital as matching their requirements.

Give the impression that you value the relationship more than the sale. Your personal mission is to do everything possible for your customers to make sure the full resources of your organisation are utilised to help them achieve *their* objectives by using your products and services. It's a problem-solving partnership.

Respect the other person's view

The secret of good listening is to listen in a way that empowers the speaker. Whenever *we* feel respected we get a warm feeling. We instinctively think better of the *other person*. We think they are smarter, more capable and more trustworthy – after all, if they see the best in us they must be very shrewd.

The better you make the customers feel about themselves, the more they will like you and trust you. The secret of getting people to like you is deceptively simple – like them first. And the secret of getting people to respect you is *respect them first*.

Be there after the sale

On sales courses we often ask participants to raise their hands if they always call their customers back after the sale. Usually around 15 to 20 per cent do. This is more than it used to be, so the message is getting through. Then we ask, why don't more of you make follow-up calls after a sale?

You can guess what most groups say: There might be a problem. The product or service might not be all the customer wanted it to be.

But that's an opportunity missed. Nothing cements the buyer–seller relationship more than the salesperson calling back or showing up in person after the sale. Always do it, especially when there's a problem. Regard it as a cardinal sin not to.

A salesperson expires suddenly and is greeted by St Peter at the Pearly Gates.

'Welcome,' says St Peter, 'and congratulations on making it here. This is a particularly good time to arrive as we've worked hard in recent months to improve our levels of customer service. We are now able to offer you two options. You can spend a day in heaven and a day in hell, and then you can decide where you want to spend eternity.'

Because a salesperson should always have an open mind, our hero was happy to sample both scenarios. First stop was hell, where the salesperson was welcomed by the devil and taken to a beautiful country hotel and leisure club. After 18 holes on the most spectacular golf course imaginable, they retired to the dining room where they were met by many of the seller's departed colleagues. Smiling and dressed in black tie, they all enjoyed a lobster dinner, vintage wines and cabaret. It was the most enjoyable evening the salesperson could remember.

He then spent the next day in heaven. And while it was nice to lounge around on the clouds and play the harp, he felt something was missing. So he went back to St Peter and said, 'I've made my choice. I want to go to hell.' St Peter obligingly put him on the elevator heading down. Again he was greeted by the devil. But this time, when the salesperson arrived he saw desolate wasteland covered in rubbish. His former friends were dressed in rags and they were picking up rubbish and putting it in sacks. 'Wait a minute!' yelled the salesperson. 'Yesterday there was a country hotel here. We ate lobster, we drank fine wines. What happened?'

The devil smiled and said, 'That's easy. Yesterday you were a prospect. Today you're a client.'

Be transparent

If you knew your action or conversation was going to be written up verbatim in tomorrow's papers, would you be proud of the way you handled it?

To be held in high regard by a customer or colleague is something that can never be demanded. You earn it through your actions.

Make your word your bond. If you say 'The proposal will be with you on Thursday morning', make sure it's there. Your customers should be able to set their watches by your reliability. Your dependability builds trust and respect.

From time to time we all need reminding that we cannot use our interpersonal skills to get us out of what our behaviour got us into. We are judged by our actions, not by our words. The best way to build trust is to be trustworthy.

Be courteous

Courtesy costs nothing but what it buys is priceless. Handling situations, especially tricky ones, in a positive, constructive way makes everyone a winner. There is a quality about courteous people that makes us trust them. If they go out of their way to be pleasant, polite and well mannered, then somehow we sense they have our interests at heart. They are more likeable and we are keen to do business with people we like.

It's especially important to apply this principle when you hear that, as sometimes happens, you have not succeeded in securing a piece of business you were pitching for. However close you were, however much time and experience the bid cost you, remain courteous. Never allow the customer to sense annoyance or irritation. Simply be constructive and find out where you didn't match up and why the decision went against you. Don't burn your bridges with people by being a bad loser, otherwise you'll miss out on future opportunities as well.

Be appreciative

Continually communicate that the relationship is not taken for granted. Send thank you notes: 'We value your business and appreciate the manner in which you conduct it.' The power of a thank you note is hard if not impossible to beat. It's ahead of the phone because the recipient knows it takes more effort. People don't forget kindness.

▶ People Buy People First

The ability to establish trust is vital to building relationships, but to be effective there is another skill to master – the way we connect with people on an individual level.

When relating to other people, don't emphasise the differences between you. Instead, emphasise the similarities, the things you agree on, feel the same way about, what you have in common.

A simple analogy exists with musical resonance. If you pluck a string on a guitar and hold it close to another guitar, the same string will begin to vibrate, even though the two don't touch. Similarly, people like people who are on their wavelength, who understand their point of view, who are agreeable, who have similar interests. Rapport is meeting people in their model of the world. It's the naturally occurring 'dance' that happens when two people get along.

Suppose you attend a course on effective presentation skills. It's quite nerve racking, but you find yourself sitting next to someone who works for a firm you know. This is the first course on the subject for both of you, and you both have to address your national sales conference later in the year. What's your reaction?

The commonality between you immediately builds interest and promotes conversation. You are like the other person in those respects and that increases the rapport between you.

Some years ago we were looking to recruit some more training consultants. A recruitment consultant I'll call Mike contacted us wanting to sell his organisation's services.

My PA was very capable. Whenever anyone called from such an agency she always said, 'Thanks for calling but we do our own recruitment.'

Mike responded, 'Fine, I can appreciate that but I have just interviewed someone who is really excited about working for your company.'

My PA replied, 'That's good to hear, but we don't use agencies for trainers. We do use them for other staff but not for training consultants. We've also just run a very successful ad and have around 80 CVs to get through.'

Most recruitment consultants who phone up and are told 'we don't use agencies' simply accept it. They bin the lead and rarely contact us again. Mike, however, was made of sterner stuff.

'I tell you what,' he said, 'if I send the CV in, could you perhaps put it on Robin's desk?'

My PA agreed, 'OK, I'll do that but I can't promise you anything.'

The CV arrived the following day and Mike was on the phone checking to make sure it had arrived. He then called every other day to check progress. This went on for about two weeks. He was a brilliant relationship builder. I am not quite sure how he did it, but he really got my PA on his side. She asked me whether I had had a chance to look at the CV yet. She was beginning to get cross, not with him for calling, but with me because I didn't get back to him.

Why didn't she get cross with him? She liked him. He had built a great rapport with her. He was extremely courteous and polite. I wish I had recorded those conversations – they must have been an object lesson in selling yourself. Mike was a master relationship builder.

We met his candidate.

▶ Building the Relationship
Summary of Main Points

If the relationship isn't there, the next sale won't be either. The one ingredient your competitors cannot copy is the relationship you have with your customer.

Think like a partner. Say to the customer, 'I'm not here to sell you this product, I'm here to be your long-term adviser.'

Trust is the precondition for loyalty. Ultimately, it is loyalty that delivers repeat business. Be superb at establishing trust.

Seven ideas for building trust:

- Be other person centred. Let people sense you have their interests at heart, not just your own.
- Represent the customer. Be bias free.
- Listening builds trust. Good selling is selling that listens.
- Be there after the sale. It bonds you to the customer.
- Be transparent.
- Be courteous, no matter what happens.
- Be appreciative.

People buy people first. Build rapport by emphasising the similarities between you.

7

Gap Analysis Selling

Widen the gap before presenting your solution and you'll win more business.

A customer who knows they have a requirement and one who doesn't present two different situations for the seller.

Your ability to **find out and match** is at the core of all selling, as we saw in Chapter 4, but it assumes that your customer *has* a requirement. What if they don't, or what if they say their company is happy with what it is doing now?

In this situation, finding the requirement is pointless – there isn't one. The only way to continue with this customer is to *create* a requirement. To achieve this, **find out** is replaced by a two-step process: *uncover* a gap and then *enlarge* it to the point where the customer wants to do something about it.

▶ Step 1 – Uncover a Gap

In all sales, in order for a customer to act, there must be a perceived gap between where they are now and where they would like to be, because it is only this gap that allows us to sell. So we are either looking for an *existing* problem/difficulty, or we are looking to *create* a drawback by showing that there is a better way.

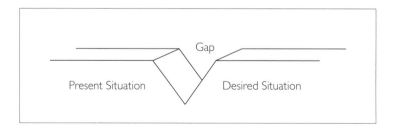

The gap can be defined as:

■ something they are no longer 100 per cent happy with
   (perhaps they were totally happy but now they're only 95 per
   cent happy)
■ a concern
■ a drawback
■ a difficulty.

Finding a gap often means we have to review our approach to sales
opportunities.

One of our clients, an international container operator, was
approached by a major European car manufacturer who needed
assistance with an eleventh-hour emergency. It wanted to ship some
heavy equipment from its factory in Northern Europe to an exhibition
taking place in South Africa. Unfortunately, its usual container company
could not meet the tight deadline involved.

Our client could, and very shrewdly it agreed to do so on one
condition. A meeting would be arranged with the car manufacturer's
senior management to discuss the possibility of a regular contract – a
highly lucrative piece of business to win. That was agreed and the deal
was done.

The container operator then sat down to plan for the crucial meeting.
Its original intention was to put together an impressive presentation to
explain all its facilities, its pricing structure, its excellent service, and the
special effort it would be willing to make to gain the account.

Their sales manager then stepped in and reminded the group that such
an approach would be unlikely to win a major piece of business; all they
would get were the crumbs. Instead, what they needed to do was to
find a gap. They had to find something the car manufacturer *was not
100 per cent happy within its existing arrangements.*

This prompted the container team into adopting a 'What will it solve?'
mindset. They brainstormed the situation and made a list of the
problems or potential problems they could solve for the car
manufacturer. They then rotated these statements into questions to ask
at the meeting.

The strategy worked and interest was high. It took some time but
eventually our client secured a significant contract.

Probing questions

Here's an exercise I often use when working with clients. You can do
it by yourself or with your colleagues. Think of one of your current
customers and brainstorm the potential problems they might have
(or the opportunities they would like to realise) that you know your
product or service can help solve. Make a list of them.

Since questions not reasons are your main persuasive skill, rotate these statements into questions. These are your initial probing questions.

As an example, imagine you sell mobile high-output projectors for use with notebook computers. What problems does this product solve?

- Projected images being washed out by high ambient light.
- Lightweight so salespeople less likely to leave it behind.
- Very silent fan so presenters don't have to talk over the noise.

Rotate these into questions:

- 'Do you have any difficulties with projected images being washed out by high ambient light?'
- 'How do you feel about your salespeople using projectors at every opportunity to build professional image?'
- 'Do your people have any concerns about having to raise their voices to talk over the noise made by cooling fans?'

Rotating benefit statements into questions is easy once you get the hang of it.

If the customer expresses interest in any of these areas run with that; otherwise go on to the next question. Keep in mind that you have a twofold objective:

- To find out what they are doing now.
- To find out what they are not 100 per cent happy with.

To support the above approach there are three general questions that are useful in helping to seek out gaps. Use your own judgement about which questions you feel comfortable with. If you feel at ease, your customer will too. Just keep in mind that your task is to find out what gaps exist in the areas where you can help. Use a conversational style, be respectful and build trust by remembering that your role is as a business consultant with the customer's interests at heart.

- **'What concerns do you have?'** Not only is this a good question to ask when you are with the customer, but it's a good way to prepare for the meeting. Think of a sales interview you have coming up in the next few days and ask yourself: 'What concerns will be on the mind of this customer?'

This is the role of empathy in selling. You put yourself in the customer's position and see the interview from their perspective.

In addition, when you are very familiar with your customer's marketplace and know the problems they encounter, you can begin probing for concerns with questions such as: 'It often happens in this industry that x occurs. Is that the case here?'

A word of caution about the interview. If you go in and ask 'Do you have a problem with this/that?', the customer will become defensive. No one likes to admit they have a problem. So it's much more effective to ask 'What concerns do you have?'

■ **'If you had a free hand to make any improvement you wanted, what would it be?'** This question, known as the magic wand or superprobe, is very useful for uncovering small gaps or wish lists with which you can subsequently work. Use it when the customer says, 'We are quite happy with our present supplier.'

Another brilliant question you can ask in this situation is: 'Are there any circumstances in which you would consider using a new supplier?'

As a training provider, we often speak to prospective clients who say, 'We are quite happy with our internal training arrangements.' My sales team know that's a cue to reply, 'Fine, I can understand that. Can I ask you, are there any circumstances in which you would consider using an external provider?'

In most cases, the customer will then indicate what requirements or wishes they have that are not currently being met. That's how the sale begins.

■ **'If there is one thing preventing you from achieving your growth objectives, what is it?'** Known as the chokepoint concept, this question probes for what is holding results back. It is a useful technique that focuses the mind.

Suppose I ask you, 'If there is one thing that is preventing you from blasting through your sales target, what is it?' What would you say? I am sure your answer would reveal a requirement of some description that you consider essential to overachieving in your job. Again, that's how the sale begins.

▶ Step 2 – Widen the Gap Before Presenting Your Solution

Once you have uncovered a gap, resist the temptation to jump in and match straight away. You have to enlarge the gap. Make it wider and deeper so that it demands attention, otherwise your customer will probably be happy to live with it.

Neil Rackham was the first to recognise this approach. In his research for SPIN selling, he analysed 35,000 sales calls over 15 years and found that the ability to build the requirement with questioning skills before presenting the solution was a key indicator of success, especially in larger sales.

I was at Victoria Station on the London Underground recently and, as the train approached, the public address system announced, 'Mind the gap.' It occurred to me that no one ever pays much attention to this, presumably because the gap is relatively small and most people are used to it.

Suppose the gap was 100 feet deep and 6 feet wide: then it would be a major gap and it would hold our attention completely. Selling is like that. If the gap in the customer's mind is relatively small, it gets little attention. The seller's job is to enlarge it, to get the customer to focus on it and realise that it's large enough to do something about.

Arguably, the biggest mistake salespeople can make in a larger sale is to begin matching small requirements.

In the early 1990s, LDL's client details were held on a card-based filing system. The mailing list was computerised but not the client file. The details of each account were held on a pre-printed A4 card.

We had 3,000 accounts on the system and 10 telephone salespeople in the department, so each handled some 300 accounts. Although the operation was entirely manual it worked effectively, provided each salesperson knew their accounts well.

We were approached by a company selling computerised sales tracking packages. Its salesperson made an appointment with our general manager. After exchanging niceties, he quite correctly began by asking questions to uncover the drawbacks in our existing operation.

■ 'How do you keep your mailing list up to date?'
■ 'How do you quickly target a particular market?'

- 'What happens when you want to write to a large number of prospective customers during a new business drive?'
- 'How do you make sure all leads are being followed up?'
- 'What happens when someone leaves?'

We freely admitted that there were drawbacks in those areas and expressed an interest in how computerisation would help.

The company presented its solution, which was very impressive. Each salesperson would have their own terminal and key information directly into the client file. They would be able to produce correspondence from standard formats and no longer have to overload our already stretched administration department. Writing to new customers would happen at the touch of a button and managers would have accurate analyses of what everyone was doing.

It was terrific, just what we wanted. If it had cost £500 we'd have bought it, if it had cost £5,000 we'd have bought it – but the system would have cost us £50,000.

However, it wasn't just the financial investment, it was the hassle and risk involved in changing from a card-based to a computerised system. Our sales team would have to learn keyboard skills. The changeover period would be a real headache, and how could we be sure that the end result would produce any more sales?

We didn't pursue the proposal. We did have a gap, we could see the benefits of computerising and we liked the salesperson, but because the system was expensive and involved hassle and risk, we decided to live with our existing system.

Where did the salesperson go wrong? He uncovered the gap, but he did not widen it. People are usually quite happy to admit to problems and shortcomings in what they are currently doing or using, but that does *not* necessarily mean they will buy. We must make them want it more. We must widen the gap to the point where the customer is no longer happy to live with it and wants to take action.

Some years later, we realised for ourselves that computerising the entire operation would be a great boon. We did so and it was one of the most successful initiatives we've ever had. We should have done it years earlier. By not using the correct skills and by not building our requirement, that first salesperson did us a great disservice.

How to widen the gap

We effectively want to *bang a wedge* into the gap to make it wider. The strategy is to investigate the two sides of the gap. In the diagram below the left-hand side is the existing situation, the 'problem' side of the gap. The right-hand side is the future situation, the 'solution' side of the gap.

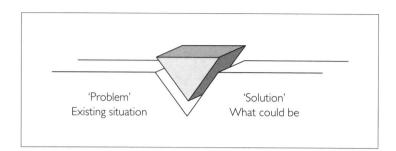

'Problem'
Existing situation

'Solution'
What could be

To widen the gap simply:

- make the problem seem more serious, more expensive and therefore more concerning.
- And then, make the solution seem more attractive and therefore worth solving.

Let's now investigate how we can achieve this gap widening.

Keep in mind, as we have said before, that questions not reasons are your main persuasive skills.

One of my colleagues, Julian Feinstein, tells a story that vividly illustrates how to use this concept. He was approached by a financial services salesman who wanted to discuss his insurance requirements.

Julian said, 'I'm up to here with insurance. I don't need any more insurance.' *Not much of a requirement here.*

The salesman replied, 'Fine, I can understand that, but allow me to review your portfolio, then I can give you some advice as to how sound your present level of cover is.'

Julian ummed and aahed, thought about it and finally agreed, 'OK, you can review my portfolio but watch my lips, I don't want to buy any more insurance.'

The salesman then proceeded to ask Julian a series of questions about his existing financial arrangements. At the end of this he conceded, 'Well, it seems you are very well covered for your retirement and your family is well protected.'

He'd been attempting to find a gap and so far hadn't succeeded. He continued, 'What is your main source of income?'

'My salary, my job.'

'I appreciate it's a fairly unlikely possibility, but what would happen if you couldn't carry on working. Where would your income come from?'

'That's easy,' said Julian. 'My company would continue to pay me for 12 months.'

'Those are excellent conditions,' commented the salesman. 'I know it's a very unlikely possibility, but what would happen if you couldn't carry on

working *after* those 12 months? Where would your income come from?'
Julian was somewhat taken aback. 'Uh, I have some shares I could sell,
some policies I could surrender. It wouldn't be easy.'
The salesman had found a gap – Julian had no income protection after
12 months.
'I know it's an unlikely possibility, but if that happened, how would it
affect your lifestyle?' asked the salesman.
'I've never really thought about it. I guess I'd have to sell my house, do
without a car – you've made your point!'
'What sort of difference would £1,000 a month make to you in those
circumstances?'
'Terrific, I'd be able to keep my house, keep a car.'
'Accepting that it's very unlikely to happen, how much would you be
willing to put aside each month to cover for that small possibility?'
'£20 to £25 a month.'
'£23 a month will buy you £1,030 worth of cover.'
What do you think Julian did? He bought the policy.

That's an example of top-class professional selling. Julian later
learned that the salesperson was a member of the elite Five Million
Dollar Round Table, which recognises the very best in the field.
Julian was also delighted with the salesman's approach and style.
He's been recounting the story ever since! It's good selling for
several reasons:

- The seller transferred his ideas through questions, so Julian
  reached his own conclusions.
- Having uncovered the gap – no income protection after 12
  months – the seller *did not* then do what 99 out of 100
  salespeople would have done, present his proposal. Instead he
  took the existing situation, the problem side of the gap, and
  widened it. The pivotal question he asked was, 'If that
  happened, how would it affect your lifestyle?'
- Note that the salesman did not *tell* Julian how it would affect
  his lifestyle: 'You wouldn't be able to pay your mortgage.
  You'd probably have to do without a car.' That would have
  been ineffective and pushy. He knew, like all good sellers, that
  questions not reasons are your main persuasive skills. Never
  tell if you can ask.
- The salesman took the solution side of the gap and widened
  that with the question, 'What sort of difference would £1,000
  a month make to you in those circumstances?' Having
  uncovered and widened the gap, the sale was easily made.

■ At all times he was courteous and had Julian's best interests at heart. That builds trust.

Let's look in more detail at how gap widening questions should be framed.

Gap analysis – the problem side

The objective is to concentrate the customer's mind on the 'problem' or 'existing situation' side of the gap. The best way to achieve this is to ask them to tell you about the drawbacks and difficulties of the existing situation:

■ 'You say your equipment is a bit slow. How is that affecting you?'
■ 'What difficulties does it cause?'
■ 'What are the knock-on effects of that?'
■ 'What problems does that produce?'
■ 'What would happen if it continued for the next 12 months?'

Always think what is going to make the customer think that the original situation is more serious than they had realised.

Gap analysis – the solution side

The next objective is to concentrate the customer's mind on the solution side of the gap. Traditional sales training says *tell* the customer the benefits. As we saw above, the new style is more effective: *ask* the customer to tell you the benefits. Ask the customer to describe the value and usefulness of solving the problem:

■ 'What do you see as the plusses of this approach?'
■ 'What difference will it make?'
■ 'If it went well, how else would it help you?'
■ 'If you could sort this out, how would it help you?'
■ 'What do you want to achieve?'
■ 'Why is that important?'

These questions are very effective because they allow people to sell themselves on the idea of going ahead. If you are thinking of joining a health club and I ask you why, you will tell me your reasons: 'I want to improve my tennis', 'I want to lose a few pounds', 'I want to meet more people'. In explaining them to me you will reinforce your desire to do them. Nothing is easier than selling someone their own idea.

▶ Gap Analysis Selling
Summary of Main Points

In every sale, in order for the customer to act, there must be a perceived gap between where they are now and where they would like to be. That's how the sale begins.

- The first step is to uncover a gap. Find something the customer is no longer 100 per cent happy with that your product or service will solve.
- Having uncovered the gap, resist the temptation to jump in and begin selling. It's too early. Instead, widen the gap. Bang a conceptual wedge into it. The gap must be large enough to justify action *before* you present your solution.
- To widen the 'problem' side of the gap, make the 'problem' seem more serious, more expensive and therefore more concerning. Use questions not reasons. *Ask* the customer to describe the drawbacks and difficulties of the existing situation.
- To widen the 'solution' side of the gap, make the 'solution' seem more attractive and therefore worth solving. *Ask* the customer to tell you the benefits of solving the problem.

8

The Art of Sales Negotiation

Negotiate agreement without sacrificing margin.

So you have identified a potential customer, built rapport with them and used your sales skills to get them to want to buy from you. But once they have decided to buy, they turn their attention to getting the best deal, the best price, the best terms. They now move to the penultimate stage of the RACERNI® buying sequence – Negotiate.

The customer you speak to on Monday morning is almost certain to have received training on how to improve the terms they get from their suppliers. The popularity of negotiating skills training for buyers has grown dramatically in recent years.

When was the last time a buyer told you they only had a certain amount in their budget? Or promised huge orders out there somewhere in the future? Or gave you static about your competition? These are negotiating tactics, just a few of the dozens of tactics the buyer has learned and probably uses at every opportunity.

It's worth remembering that not all buyers want partnerships. Some are quite happy with transactional relationships and will negotiate terms strongly. And those who do extol the virtues of buyer/seller partnerships want to negotiate most of the profit from such arrangements for themselves. Put another way, they may talk win-win, but what they really want is WIN-win: a big win for them and a little win for us.

In a sales negotiation, your objective is to reach agreement without sacrificing margin. The overriding secret is to negotiate in a way that leaves both parties *satisfied with the final agreement*. What follows are seven techniques to help you. Weave them into your everyday transactions and you'll make yourself a better, more profitable negotiator.

▶ I – Recognise the Price Challenge

One of the techniques buyers learn early in their careers is the 'flinch'. On learning the price, they react with a sharp intake of breath and say:

- 'What!' or
- 'You must be joking' or
- 'I had no idea you were talking about that kind of money' or
- 'We've had a very good quotation from one of your competitors and some of my colleagues are leaning in that direction.'

These are all negotiating ploys, designed to lower your aspirations and set you up for a discount. Some buyers are so skilled in this area that they deserve an Oscar nomination. They may be bursting to buy from you, they may be completely 'sold' on your solution, but they still have a go at your price. Why? It's their job. They are paid to do that.

We'd like a discount please

Here's another cry from the heart: *don't be a price crumbler.*

The buyer says, 'We'd like a discount please.'

The seller responds, 'OK, since you're a new customer, as a gesture of goodwill we'll give you 8 per cent.'

That's not being a negotiator, that's being a wimp! Anyone can give the profit margin away. Some people are so used to crumbling that they mention discount before they mention price. Be proud of your price.

Your first response to the buyer's price challenge should be to defend your price persistently. Persuade the buyer that the benefits of the solution as quoted still justify acceptance.

Simply put, when the buyer says 'You've got to be joking at that price', your response should be 'No, I'm not joking, look at what you get. You get this . . . and this . . . and this . . .' What you are really saying is, 'Mr Customer, your negotiating ploy isn't working here – we're not going to crumble on price.'

In many cases, solidly defending your price is enough to achieve agreement. But what if it's not? What if the buyer persists in their demands and it becomes obvious that you are going to have to concede something?

The answer is at the heart of negotiation: don't just give it away, trade it.

▶ 2 – If a Concession Is Necessary, Trade It

If you ask people to define negotiation they usually reply 'giving just enough away to buy agreement'. However, giving things away doesn't buy agreement. It usually only convinces the other party how easily we can be taken for a ride. They begin to think about what else they can get from you.

If you concede when I press you, what's my best bet? . . . to press again.

That type of behaviour is not negotiating. Negotiation means we *both* move. In Chapter 4 we defined the core of selling as **find out and match**. The equivalent core of negotiation is **what I offer you, balanced by what you offer me**.

It is to be hoped that you're not reading this chapter to improve your skills at giving things away. You're reading it to develop your negotiating skills, and that means mutual movement. If you *have* to move towards the other party, you must *insist* that they move towards you as well. Nothing, absolutely nothing, is given away for free.

Also beware the common delusion that the buyer will recognise a good competitive offer and deal with it as such. Part of their satisfaction comes from playing the game well, from their enjoyment of the negotiation process.

Here are some techniques for trading concessions.

If you . . . then we can . . .

This phrase is an excellent, tried-and-tested method of exploring negotiable areas and avoiding unilateral concessions. The concept is mutual movement. If you *move towards us*, then we can *move towards you*.

Here's an example of how it works. The buyer says, 'We'd like a discount please.'

You reply, 'We can't afford to discount as things stand, however, *if you* were to increase your order from three to four units, *then we can* agree a 5 per cent discount. How does that sound?'

You are effectively offering the buyer a concession without taking your hands off it. If you get nothing in return, you simply take it back.

Here are some more examples that illustrate the approach:

■ 'If you feel able to increase your commitment from 6 to
12 months (or let us have a sole supplier relationship, or be a

reference site or whatever), then I'm sure we can get closer to your investment figure.'

■ 'If you pay by the 10th, we can guarantee no price increase.'
■ 'If you waive on-site inspection, we can meet your completion date.'

Let's split the difference

How often have you heard that one? How many times have you fallen for it?

Let's create a scenario. In return for a £10,000 order, you are willing to trade a 5 per cent discount. Your customer comes back with, 'That's not enough, we want 10 per cent.'

What do you do? It's tempting to say, 'Tell you what we'll do, let's split the difference and agree at 7.5 per cent. How does that sound?'

If you do that, you've just given a further 2.5 per cent away without getting anything in return. That's not negotiating.

But what happens when the *buyer* uses the 'let's split the difference' line on you? If you accept it, once again you are giving away 2.5 per cent with nothing in return.

As an alternative say, 'I can't afford to, but I tell you what we can do – if you agree to (whatever your required concession is), then we can agree at 7.5 per cent. How does that sound?'

Is that negotiable?

Imagine you sell telecommunications solutions and you are making your final presentation to the board of a call centre provider. It's a major proposal, and when you have finished the managing director smiles and comments, 'This looks to be a very impressive solution. However, before we go any further, may I ask you about the £56,000 price you have quoted? Is that negotiable?'

The customer is testing the price. That's a perfectly reasonable thing for an intelligent executive to do. How do you handle it?

Let's look at the options. If you say 'no', it sounds very strong. It also invariably sounds like a form of attack. That tends to hurt the relationship by making people feel they are being pushed around. You may also lose the business on the price objection, so this response is to be avoided.

On the other hand, if you say 'yes', your price is going to be reduced for sure. You are sounding weak and a skilled negotiator will gleefully take advantage of that.

A terrific phrase that has helped thousands of sellers is to reply,

'We are always willing to listen to any constructive ideas that will improve the acceptability of our proposals.'

You haven't said 'no' and you haven't said 'yes'. Instead you are leaving the door open for further discussion. That's a hallmark of a mature negotiator. Your answer has the consultative-partner style stamped all over it and is one of the most professional skills you can use.

Your customer will probably respond 'What sort of constructive ideas?', to which you say, 'If you agree to x then we can agree to y.' Then you are straight into a normal negotiation.

▶ 3 – Understand Aspiration Levels

There is an old negotiating maxim: aim high and you'll get more.

Consider Mary, a senior sales executive with a software development company, who is preparing for a key presentation. She says to herself, 'This is an extremely important sale for me. I must get this business. I really believe we have a superb solution for the customer. I'll get the quoted price with standard terms and conditions. If they really push me I might possibly concede up to 2 per cent, though they'll have to push really hard.' Mary understands that some small movement is part of the commercial process.

Contrast that with George, who is preparing for a similar presentation and says to himself, 'This is an extremely important piece of business. I really must do everything to get it. If I have to, I'll concede 20 per cent on the price.'

Who will negotiate the best deal?

Mary's mindset, her aspiration level, is way ahead of George's. She understands that the person who aims high gets more.

Our aspirations can be defined as what we *expect* to get. They reflect our intended goal. Aspirations move up and down with the tide of success. If things are going well, if you're feeling strong and you've got lots of leverage, then your aspirations rise. You expect more, which almost always means you get more. However, if things are *not* going so well, you're not feeling strong and you seem to have little leverage, then your aspirations fall. You expect less and get less.

It's a fact of life that our expectations and our achievements are inextricably linked. Consequently, a major part of any negotiation is to *lower* the other side's aspiration level.

When the buyer talks of budget restrictions or shows surprise at the price, they are lowering your aspirations. Some buyers will begin lowering your aspirations a year before they place their order!

Here's an upside-down example to illustrate the way aspirations work.

Imagine you sell management consultancy and, during a presentation, you are told that your competitors' prices are a lot *higher* than yours. What would your reaction be? Would you want to raise or reduce your price?

You'd want to raise it. Do you see the implication? Your aspirations go up and down depending on what you are *told* once you are in contact with the other person. Everything said affects the price in the other person's head.

Allowing time to pass is another highly effective way of lowering aspirations. The party most constrained by time is weaker. Time and patience are power in negotiation. Ask anyone who has worked in the Far East or Russia – those countries understand that 'let them sweat' leads to concession after concession.

▶ 4 – Be Stingy!

When you offer a concession, obey the golden rule: Make the buyer work harder for it. Trade concessions reluctantly and one by one. Call a concession a concession. People put greater value on things that are hard to get.

Being stingy is an excellent tactic because it helps the other party to believe that they've reached the bottom line. That's good for their self-respect.

Negotiating training relates to almost everything we do. For example, let's suppose you decide to sell your flat or house. You put it on the market for £115,000. After several weeks you receive an offer of £110,000, which is the figure you had in mind when you agreed the asking price with the agent.

What's your reaction to the offer? More than likely you say, 'Great, I'll take it.' You are delighted you've sold the house at the price you wanted. You have a celebratory drink with your partner and retire to bed. But for some reason you don't sleep very well. Over and over you have the thought, 'I agreed too quickly, I should have asked for more. I'm a lousy negotiator.'

Do you see what's wrong here? When we say 'yes' too quickly, we think we're a lousy negotiator because we may have left some money on the table.

Let's now consider the same sale from the buyer's viewpoint. She has been looking for a house in your area. She sees yours and makes an offer £5,000 less than the asking price. You agree. The buyer is pleased, returns home and, like you, doesn't sleep very well. Over and over she is thinking, 'He said yes too quickly. I should have offered less. Oh, I'm a lousy negotiator.'

This is a crucial point – when we agree too quickly, *both* sides later think they are lousy negotiators.

When negotiating, the worst thing you can do to the other party is not to insult them or go over their head – it's to accept their first offer. Doing so damages both parties' satisfaction with the deal.

This approach translates into one of my favourite negotiating rules of thumb: whenever you are about to say yes to a deal, say *no* one more time.

▶ 5 – Look for Negotiable Variables

As we have seen, the core of negotiation is: *what I offer you balanced by what you offer me.* What we offer each other when trading concessions are referred to as our negotiable variables. They are the ammunition of our bargaining skills. And this brings up another key point: it doesn't matter how good we are at negotiation, we need lots of these variables to trade effectively.

The challenge here is to stop seeing price as *the* issue. Price is *an* issue, it shouldn't be *the* issue.

All the variables in and around the agreement can be used to improve it. Once you start looking beyond haggling over the price, you can begin to put some excellent agreements together.

For example, imagine that a customer says she loves your product, but will only go ahead at a 10 per cent discount. You also know from previous discussions that she requires the product quickly for use in two different locations. How could you handle this without dropping the price?

A simple solution is to say, 'Instead of a discount, what if we ship directly to each of your locations by the end of next week?'

'It's a deal,' is likely to be the reply.

You have reached agreement and the cost to you is much less than a discount. That's what win-win is all about.

How many variables do you have?

When we conduct in-company training, clients often tell us that they don't have that many negotiable variables. We then spend up to two hours of course time working with them, brainstorming possibilities.

Invariably they surprise themselves and end up with a list of 20 or 30 variables. That alone transforms the quality of their negotiated agreements.

Here's an exercise I'd like you to do now. Take a few minutes and make a list of all your negotiable variables. Other than price, what could you trade?

If your list is a short one, start from the other end and list those sacred constants you never negotiate – maybe, just maybe, some of those could become variables. Remember, the more variables you have, the better you will negotiate.

When making this list, keep in mind that it's not just what you have to offer the buyer, it's what you would like from them. Perhaps they collect, perhaps they provide part of it themselves, perhaps they give you a guarantee of work during your quiet period. What would tempt you into giving them a better deal?

▶ 6 – Know How to Handle Deadlock

If you are deadlocked with the buyer, point out the time invested by *both* sides before admitting defeat: 'John, we've both invested a great deal of time in this, let's go through it one more time before we admit defeat.' It's not just your time, but the buyer's as well.

Recognise that no one likes to admit defeat. So when deadlock seems imminent, debate, verbalise, explore and discuss the situation and just maybe some other hook will emerge. You then grab it and away you go.

The edge of the cliff

A word of warning. Sometimes a buyer will deliberately deadlock in order to lower your aspirations. She will take you to the edge of the cliff and see how tough you talk then. Buyers know that some sellers are so terrified of deadlock that, at the first sign, they will make concessions rather than face the possibility of not closing the business.

The well-trained buyer exploits this fear by threatening deadlock: 'Well, if that's the best you can do, it's outside what I'm allowed to spend, so we'll have to pass on it this time.'

The unskilled seller responds by offering a discount, and then rationalises it: 'It's the only way we could get the business.'

The skilled seller responds by suggesting another look before we admit defeat, or perhaps an alternative package. This latter response is discussed later.

A little overeager

Whether you are acting as the seller or the buyer, if you have pushed the other side too far and deadlock looms, you must have the grace to renegotiate. The all-time best line here is: 'I may have been a little overeager, let's go through it one more time before we admit defeat.' The word 'overeager' allows you to climb down.

I learned this many years ago from an outstanding salesman, Clive Holmes. I happened to be in his office when he was on the phone negotiating to buy a horse from an owner in Ireland. The horse was advertised for sale at £12,000. Clive made a low offer and clearly, from what I could hear of the conversation, the owner was outraged. Clive had pushed too hard.

Then, with great grace and aplomb, he said, 'My apologies, I may have been a little overeager, can we start again?' He bought the horse close to the asking price and I learned a valuable lesson: if your stance in a transaction is to test the other party by aiming high, you must be a master of the gracious climbdown, otherwise you both walk away lose-lose. Anyone can be a tough negotiator; the object is to be effective.

▶ 7 – Know How to Handle the Buyer Who Says 'I Like Your Proposal, But This Is All I've Got'

This is a brilliant buyer's skill, the undisputed crown jewel. In fact, if this chapter was written solely for buyers, I'd urge you to take the tactic on board as one of the finest available anywhere. To explain why it's such a good buyer's skill, consider the two parts of the tactic:

- 'I like your proposal' is effectively saying, 'I like you, I like your company, I like your product, I like your service, I like your pricing.'
- 'But this is all I've got' – there is an implied budget restriction.

So how do we react? Let's take the all-important phrase, 'I like your proposal'. We all want to be liked. Here we think we're nine-tenths of the way there. Our reaction is, 'I've got a live one here, now what do I have to do to close the business?' Unfortunately, for too many of us this usually becomes, 'What do I have to *give away* to win the business?'

Buyers know that an unskilled seller will respond to this tactic by offering a discount. A good seller, on the other hand, will respond by discussing alternatives. Then the buyer *learns more* about what they are buying, so either way the buyer wins.

The way to handle this tactic is to have alternatives available. The buyer must be made to realise that if they want to change the price, you will change the package. For the quoted price there is one package; for another price, there is another package.

To pull this off successfully, the secret is to have the alternatives thought through in advance. You then know exactly which package to offer.

Above all, the strength of this countermeasure lies in its inherent ability to flush out whether the phrase 'this is all I've got' is a *real* budget restriction or simply a negotiating ploy.

Reverse the roles

To illustrate how this works, reverse the roles and imagine you are part of a buying team with the job of purchasing much needed new office equipment.

You draw up a detailed specification and contact six suppliers. After receiving proposals from each and carefully evaluating which best meets your requirements, you decide to award the business to Ace Systems. In their proposal they have quoted a price of £31,500. Your managing director *agrees the funding* and gives you the green light to proceed, but says, 'Do everything you can to get the price down.'

You call Alison, the business development manager from Ace Systems, back in and say to her, 'We like your proposal, it's just what we want, but we've only got £27,000 available. How can you help?'

She responds by offering an alternative package that does not meet all your criteria. How interested are you going to be in this alternative? Not very, I think you'll agree.

Now imagine a different scenario. This time your managing director has given you an *actual* budget of £27,000, and that's as high as you can go. You use the same approach: 'We've only got £27,000. How can you help?' Alison again responds with an alternative package. How interested are you this time? *Very* interested.

Can you see how to use this to your advantage? As a seller you effectively have a way of finding out whether the buyer's tactic is real or a ploy.

When the customer says 'We like your proposal but we only have £27,000 available', you respond by offering an alternative package and gauging their interest in it. *If they don't have much interest, it's almost certainly a ploy.* Your response has uncovered that they do have slack in their budget.

However, if they *are* interested, it's more likely to be a genuine budget restriction. Once you know which, it's much easier to adjust your response.

Negotiation is a game; a serious game, but a game nonetheless. Learn the rules and go for it. And make sure you take notes during your discussions. The dullest pencil works better than the sharpest memory.

▶ The Art of Sales Negotiation Summary of Main Points

Good negotiation leaves both parties satisfied with the final agreement. Keep these essentials in mind:

1. *Recognise the price challenge or 'flinch'.* Don't be a price crumbler. Your first response to the buyer's price challenge is to defend your price persistently.
2. *If a concession is necessary, trade it* – what I offer you balanced by what you offer me. If you have to move towards the other party, you must insist they move towards you as well.
3. *Understand aspiration levels.* Aspirations are what we expect to get. The person who aims high gets more. Our aspirations move up and down depending on how things are going and what we are told by the other party.
4. *Be stingy!* People put greater value on things that are hard to get. Agreeing too quickly undermines both buyer's and seller's confidence in the agreement.
5. *Look for negotiable variables.* Stop seeing price as the issue. All the variables in and around the deal can be used to improve it.
6. *Know how to handle deadlock.* Point out the time invested by both sides before admitting defeat. Master the gracious climbdown. 'I may have been a little overeager, let's go through it one more time before we admit defeat.'
7. *Respond to 'I like your proposal, but this is all I've got' by offering an alternative package and gauging the other's interest in it.* If they don't have much interest, it's usually a ploy.

9
Major Account Selling

To handle major accounts you need additional skills.

Like most salespeople, you probably started out making relatively small sales. You worked hard learning about your products or services and how to sell them. You worked on yourself and achieved significant success. You were then asked to manage one or more of your company's major accounts. These are valuable, not just because of the revenue they produce, but because of the prestige, testimonials and references they provide for your company.

If this hasn't happened to you yet, it almost certainly will in the future. In almost every sector of business, major accounts are contributing an ever-increasing percentage of a supplier's business. It's no longer the 80/20 rule, it's 95/5.

The drawback is that when you move into major account sales, the usual small-ticket selling skills are no longer sufficient. The major sale is more complex. You are expected to quantify your proposals. You go from single to multiple decision makers, most of the selling takes place when you're not there, you make more calls on the account, the sale takes more time, and risk and competitive issues take on more significance.

To succeed in this arena there are additional skills and insights that must be mastered. This chapter looks at two rules that make a real difference. Many salespeople have transformed their approach and effectiveness by applying these powerful principles.

▶ Rule I – Sell Profit Improvement
You will almost certainly have heard the phrase 'sell the sizzle not the steak'. However, if you want to sell a truckload of steak, you must sell the financial performance, the return on investment (ROI), of buying that truckload.

Moving from small sales to major sales requires a shift in emphasis. You are no longer a salesperson selling products and services. You must talk business. You must talk the language of the boardroom: money, profits, the big picture.

In any major sale there will be three levels in the customer's organisation and your message must be positioned to suit each level.

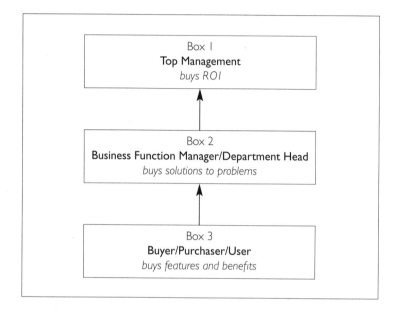

- Box 3 – This first level is the buyer or user of your product/service. What do these people buy?

  They buy products and services, they are interested in features and benefits, and price versus performance comparisons. Basic sales skills are focused on this level. New salespeople spend a lot of time learning about selling matching benefits.
- Box 2 – Moving up the organisation we come to middle managers. These are the business function managers or department heads.

  They buy solutions to problems. Function managers are surrounded by problems, concerning people, productivity, manufacturing, quality, inventory, IT, sales or image. They want relief from their problems. They want their costs reduced and they want greater opportunities for more sales and greater productivity.

■ Box 1 – Most sales training focuses on the first two levels. However, the major sale usually involves Box 1, top management.

These people buy financial performance, return on investment (ROI). They are concerned with profit. They have their eyes on the big picture. The large sale almost always involves these people. To sell here you must see yourself as a salesperson selling *solutions with a good ROI.*

Whatever you do, don't waste your time selling features and benefits in the boardroom. What would happen if I spoke to your managing director about the nuts-and-bolts features of a major training programme? Their eyes would probably glaze over. To sell effectively at this level, you must talk about the financial performance of investing in training.

The mindset for major sales is profits not products. Every successful big-ticket salesperson sells the same thing: improved profits.

Improving the customer's profits means one of two things:

■ reducing costs, or
■ increasing revenue.

Think carefully about what you sell and decide whether you want to position your solution as a cost reducer or a revenue enhancer – or both. Profit improvement is the ultimate benefit.

If you present your solution as a profit improver it gives your customer an unassailable reason to proceed. As the saying goes, money doesn't talk, it shouts. Simply put, if you are able to demonstrate that your solution is an investment with a very rapid return, it's easier to move the sale forward. Sales insistence replaces sales resistance.

Adding value

Most managers understand the importance of adding value, but are confused about what the term actually means. In the small sale, you can define value as 'the product/service matches the customer's requirements at a competitive price'. Therefore adding value is *exceeding* the customer's requirement. It answers the question: 'What more can you do for me today?' A typical added-value checklist might include the following:

- technical hotlines
- training
- marketing assistance
- product development
- delivery guarantee
- returns and repairs
- communications management
- merchandising programmes
- advertising support
- customer base research
- on-line ordering

These are all valuable, and I'm sure your organisation focuses on adding value to what you sell and then stressing the benefits of these services to your customers. This approach works well up to and including middle managers, but top management wants quantification of the value you add to their business.

> 'A premium return to the customer is all the justification you need to require a premium investment.'
>
> Mack Hanan, *Key Account Selling*

The secret in the major sale is to concentrate on adding value for the *customer* rather than to the product.

What does this look like at close range? We've seen that value in the small sale is matching the customer's requirement at a competitive price. In the large sale, value is one thing and one thing only – return on investment. It equates to the ability to improve the customer's bottom line.

Words are the language of the small sale; *numbers* are the language of the major sale. Talking about value added without quantification lacks impact. It's a sideshow that doesn't matter. Salespeople who shy away from talking numbers and discuss 'improved productivity' or 'ease of use' or 'low maintenance' without quantifying its value add nothing to a major sales dialogue.

Show me the numbers

In the Tom Cruise movie, *Jerry Maguire*, Cuba Gooding Jr won an Oscar nomination for his electric performance around the 'Show me the money' punchline.

Change this to 'Show me the numbers' and you have the key to major sales.

That's something I can sell

Think about how you approach a major sale. If you're anything like me you target your efforts on the relevant departmental manager: head of IT, head of manufacturing, head of finance. However, if one of these managers has a proposal that requires funding, who is their only source of funds? Box 1 – top management.

To get funding or sign-off for your proposal, your customer must create what is essentially an investment proposal. She invites her Box 1 manager to fund her in return for growing those funds at a rate greater than or equal to the minimum threshold of what is acceptable. In practice, this means that your customer must be skilled at selling financial performance, not just operating performance, to her boss.

Your task is to help her put this proposal together. You want her reaction to be, 'That's something I can sell upstairs.' Working with your customer to put together the financial case for going ahead is the supreme act of partnership. You are selling *with* her not *to* her.

You are probably thinking that's easier said than done. Major account selling isn't easy, but hang in there, there's always a way.

The power of one

What follows is one of my all-time favourites for hooking the customer's initial interest in the major sale. It's called *the power of one*.

You say to the customer:

- 'Let's assume we can increase your sales by 1 per cent'
- 'Let's assume we can reduce your costs in this area by 1 per cent'
- 'Let's assume that as a result of this your team will effectively gain one more day each month'

One has the power of credibility. Most customers will readily agree that they can improve performance, reduce costs or increase profits by 1 per cent. It grabs their attention. It allows you to talk numbers immediately. If you can make your case assuming only a 1 per cent improvement, it's highly persuasive.

▶ Rule 2 – Cover the Bases

To succeed in a major sale we must make lots of contacts and talk to lots of people within the account. One of the ways customers reduce risk is to ensure that as many of their people as possible are in favour of the decision. This means that we must avoid the usual approach of building the sale around those we have known the longest, or can contact most easily, or who like us the most, and ignoring everyone else.

In any large sale there are multiple influencers, blockers and helpers. Each of these buyers must be identified and analysed.

Last year a senior salesperson at one of our key clients took 11 months completing a sale that involved 18 different decision makers, each with the potential to say no. Having more buyers complicates the process and lengthens the sales cycle.

No two accounts are the same and no organisation chart can tell you who the real decision makers are. You need to build up a network within the organisation to help you find out and breathe life into your approach.

Think of a sale you're working on now. Ask yourself who the key players are. Who has the ear of top management? Who must you get on your side? What are the politics? How do you analyse all of these people?

According to Bob Miller and Stephen Heiman's work on *Strategic Selling*, it is widely accepted that the best way to map the account is to analyse the people in terms of the *roles* they play in the purchase. Typically there is one financial buyer, several user buyers, an internal adviser and perhaps a consultant.

The financial buyer

This is usually one person who has the authority to release funds for this purchase. The role will move up and down the organisation, depending on perceived risk.

If risk issues are high for the customer then the financial buyer will probably be top management. However, if risk issues are smaller, it could be a departmental manager or even a user manager.

A common mistake when planning the entry strategy for a major sale is to go straight to the financial buyer. This approach comes from sales training, which stresses that you should always see the ultimate decision maker. This is fine for small sales because the ultimate decision maker is further down the organisation, but for major sales it is not always sound advice.

What do you say when you're there? Let's take an extreme example to make this point. Suppose you have targeted ICI as a potential account. Through dazzling telephone skills you get an appointment with the chief executive. There you are in front of his desk – what are you going to say? 'We've got the best product, the best terms, the best service – buy from us!'

Your embarrassment would be acute. As a rule, don't stand in front of top management until you've got *numbers* to indicate how you can improve their business.

I know many of you will be thinking of exceptions to this where calling at the top has worked and does work. There are always exceptions, but if you examine them with an open mind, they usually only work when we have very convincing information to present, or a rock solid referral, or the customer is a smaller business.

The user buyers

Top management are pushing decision making further down the organisation, as a result of both empowerment and the delayering of organisations. In addition, no managing director wants to make a major purchase without the support and cooperation of those who will use it. So as well as the financial buyer you must talk to the user buyers, the people within the account who will use or manage the use of your product or service.

User buyers are *very* important. They have to like your product/service, cooperate with it, agree with it and learn to use it. They may not have much authority, but they have a great deal of influence.

Be tuned into users. They will be asked what they think and want before any major decision is taken. Ignore them at your peril.

The internal adviser

So far so good, but the mere fact that you have played the game well up to this point doesn't mean you can rest easy, because now along comes the inevitable internal adviser.

This is the person or persons within the account who will make recommendations to the financial and user buyers. They will make judgements about the quality and suitability of your product and services. Their role is to provide advice about the best solution. They can't say yes but they can say no.

> About 12 years ago my company attempted to sell a sales programme to a major brewery. We targeted the sales director, identified his requirements and presented our solution. He seemed delighted, but we didn't get the business.
> Some time afterwards we realised our error. No one had spoken to the brewery training manager, who felt slighted at not being involved. We had naturally assumed that the sales director was the one to convince and had overlooked his internal advisers. We learned a valuable lesson and now always ask ourselves the question, 'Who will the decision maker turn to internally for advice?' Someone must cover that base.

The consultant

Consultancy is booming. Organisations have slimmed down to such an extent that expertise in certain areas is no longer available internally. Instead it is hired in when required. Consultants are frequently asked to assist companies with important purchases.

However, many salespeople treat consultants poorly. I recall a consultant attending one of our big-ticket workshops who stood up and told the group that salespeople usually treated him badly, with a looking down their nose, 'Who are you?' kind of attitude.

I asked him what would happen if salespeople asked for his help. He said, 'They'd be miles ahead of their competition.'

The best way to handle a consultant is to use what is affectionately referred to as a pre-emptive strike. Call them, meet them and ask for their help and guidance *early* in the sale. That way they feel they don't have to come back at the end and justify their existence by saying 'No!'.

Power base selling

If there is one secret to major account selling, it's 'sell to the key influencers'. Who in the account has real clout? Who has the hammer? Who are the politically powerful people that top management listen to? Where is the power base?

In his book *Power Base Selling*, Jim Holden makes the point that those who drive organisations have to create a support structure, a network of influential individuals on whom they rely to help them grow and steer the business. This is their power base.

These people are not found in the formal organisation structure, which simply depicts authority. They are found in the informal influence structure, which the salesperson must uncover. As Holden comments, 'Although there is a formal chain of command, upper management sometimes bypasses it to reach down and seek the opinion of other influencers.'

It is vital to appreciate that not everyone with authority has influence. A new CEO may have inherited a weak marketing director and not pay much attention to their contribution, so selling to that marketing director would be fruitless.

Holden observes that unlike authority, influence is usually invisible except in times of change. This provides an excellent key to unlock the power base.

Ask people in the account what happened when things changed in the past. Which people played a major role? How were decisions made? Who was given recognition? Who was promoted?

A history of past buying patterns is also a good indication of how people will buy in the future.

▶ Major Account Selling Summary of Main Points

There are two rules of major account selling:

- **Rule 1 – Sell profit improvement**. Making major sales requires a shift in emphasis. You are no longer a salesperson selling products and services – you must talk business, talk the language of the boardroom, money, profits, the big picture. Major sales involve top management and they buy financial performance.

  Quantification is king. In major sales you must strive to answer two questions: How much is it costing us? How much more could we make? Words are the language of the small sale; numbers are the language of the major sale. You must move profits, not just products and services, to your customer.

  To get numbers, offer numbers first. Use the power of *one*. This has the power of credibility. If you can make your case assuming only a 1 per cent improvement, it's highly persuasive.

- **Rule 2 – Cover the bases**. In any large sale there are multiple influencers, blockers and helpers. The best way to map the account is to analyse the people in terms of the roles they play in the purchase:

- *The financial buyer.* This is usually one person who has the authority to release funds for this purchase.
- *The user buyers.* Those in the account who will use or supervise the use of your product or service. Users are very important.
- *The internal adviser.* The person or persons within the account who will make recommendations to the financial and user buyers.
- *The consultant.* Consultants are frequently used to assist with important purchases. Ask for their input and guidance early in the sale.

10
The Complete Selling Sequence

Use the LACPOMAC® model to optimise your selling effectiveness and keep you on track.

Chapter 4 outlined the four basic steps of the sales process. The **find out and match** concept can also be expanded into a more advanced eight-stage process that can significantly improve your selling effectiveness.

This model – LACPOMAC® – will provide you with a profound insight into how to structure the face-to-face element of consultative-partner selling. It's like driving your car with a clear windscreen – it's a lot easier when you can see what you're doing.

The model looks into the detailed 'nuts and bolts' of the sales interaction, with the focus firmly on the customer's perspective – their concerns, their requirements and their priorities.

▶ The Eight Stages of LACPOMAC®

The LACPOMAC® structure, like all modern selling skills, is designed not to be followed with unbending rigidity, but to provide you with confidence and an underlying system of questions to move the sale forward.

The best salespeople I've met don't have a whole range of techniques. They ask the right questions. They know how to listen. And they have a sales model that makes sense, which they use as a navigational tool. That's the role of LACPOMAC®.

The technique involves the following steps:

1. **Lead** the conversation to focus on the customer's requirements.
2. **Ask** about the buying criteria and what the buyer believes the successful supplier will have achieved, demonstrated or

established to win the order. Uncover and widen the gap as necessary.

3. **Confirm** that the list of requirements is complete (and, if appropriate, will form the basis of the brief or tender for all suppliers involved).

4. **Pre-close** by seeking confirmation that if all the requirements are met the order will go ahead.★

5. **Order of importance** of the key buying criteria, wants and desires.★

6. **Match** the benefits, features and solutions provided by your product or service to the requirements of the buyer and **tick** off each one in turn.

7. **Ask back** before the final proposal is submitted to confirm that all of the requirements have been dealt with.

8. **Close** the sale. Submit your proposal and ask for the business.

★These are optional stages that you can use if you feel they are appropriate.

▶ Stage I – Lead

This is the lead in to the sale and reminds you that it is your responsibility to take the initiative at the beginning of the meeting, to give it structure, direction and purpose. It is also an opportunity to warm the customer up with an opening benefit or credentials statement.

If the customer has high interest, then right away ask, 'Would you mind if I asked you one or two very straightforward questions to establish whether or not we can be of any assistance to you?'

If this is a first or early meeting in the sales process and interest is not yet high, it is useful to start off with a meeting purpose statement. For instance, 'May I suggest that as this is an introductory meeting, I begin with a brief overview of our business and then perhaps you could give me a thumbnail sketch of yours. How does that sound?' (This can be compared to the 'open' stage in the four-stage process outlined in Chapter 4.)

The customer is likely to agree, because he or she can then sit back and listen to you while the meeting warms up and he can get the measure of you. There are two important things to remember here. First, your introductory statement should be short, five minutes at most, and more importantly focused on what your business is designed to achieve for your customers and what differentiates you from other suppliers.

Secondly, the customer is listening to you but at the same time thinking about how he will describe his business when it is his time to speak. You will find that if you mention, for example, your firm's turnover, employee numbers and locations, the customer will provide you with similar information in his thumbnail sketch. You can use this technique to help establish the information you require from him.

Once this exchange is complete, you can then ask, 'Would it be OK if I were to ask a few straightforward questions to understand more about your business and your requirement?'

If the signals are strong and positive, proceed to Stage 2.

▶ Stage 2 – Ask

This is the vital **find out** or fact find stage on which everything is subsequently built. The objective is to produce a *written* set of criteria on which the purchase decision will be made, that you know you can subsequently match. Sales skills built around a list of the customer's criteria are known as 'criteria for ordering' techniques.

Too many salespeople make the mistake of just collecting background facts at this stage. While this may be interesting for the seller, it is tedious for the customer.

As discussed in Chapter 4, this is where we ask the **find out** questions that probe for the customer's requirements:

- ■ 'What are you looking for?'
- ■ 'What factors are important to you?'
- ■ 'Where are you going?'
- ■ 'What do you want to achieve?'

The customer begins talking and you say, 'I'd like to jot these down.'

The importance of Stage 2 – Ask is crucial, as you'll see in the following story a delegate at one of my seminars told me.

Her advertising agency was keen to win a trendy motorcycle account, so their first meeting with the client consisted of the ad agency's top sales team, headed by their highly -experienced client services director. He and his account team opened with a short, impressive credentials presentation, then the meeting moved on to Stage 2 – Ask.

Questions were asked, but ones that only produced facts not requirements. For example, the client services director asked 'What's so special about your motorcycles?' The answer was 'Their quality – they are built to last a long time.' No questions were asked about how the client wanted their motorcycles to be seen. Nor were any questions asked to establish where the prospect wanted to be a year or two from now.

The uncomfortable client managing director agreed to let the agency do a creative presentation, based on the information shared at that meeting. The creative work presented, although imaginative and professional, got an instant 'thumbs down'. 'But why?' asked the client services director. 'Because your creative work only pushes the quality of our motorcycles. The reason people buy them is versatility. Our motorcycles can be both road and off-road bikes.' 'You never said that,' the client services director explained. 'You never asked,' the managing director replied. The meeting was over and so was the opportunity.

Probing questions normally produce a list of the customer's requirements expressed in solution terms – he wants it to do this and this and that. In listing these requirements, you should be thinking about which ones you have a good match for and which will require modifying, refining, clarifying and defining more precisely.

If the customer has no requirements or ones that are only partially built, then create and enlarge them using the gap analysis techniques discussed in Chapter 7.

Either way, you arrive at an initial specification. Your job now is to take this and construct a set of formalised criteria for ordering that you can match, better than any other supplier.

As outlined in Chapter 3, the three steps of reinforcing, shaping/guiding/modifying and adding USPs take the customer's requirement and produce a written set of criteria that you know you can match. This is a solid and professional foundation for the sale.

Note that at no time do you mention anything about your product or service; that comes later. The core structure of selling, as we have said, is **find out and match**. *It isn't find out a bit, match a bit, find out a bit more, match a bit more.* If you are going through establishing the customer's criteria and he brings up a point at which you are superb, resist the temptation to start matching. By all means say, 'I think you'll find we're very good at that', but leave the matching to its proper place *after* all the criteria have been established and agreed.

▶ Stage 3 – Confirm

You now confirm that the list of criteria is a *complete* list of everything the customer requires. This checks that you have reached the end of **finding out**.

One of the strengths of LACPOMAC® is its ability to help you check where you are in the sale. That's good for both buyer and seller.

> Seller: 'This looks a fairly comprehensive list. Is there anything else you feel is important or have we covered everything?'
> Buyer: 'That's everything.'

You then draw a line under the list of criteria.

In the unlikely event that the customer says no at the **confirm** stage, loop back and find out what other requirements he has, modify them, with his agreement, and add them to the list. It is crucial that this list is complete. Keep going back until it is.

When the list is **confirmed**, you have agreement that **finding out** is complete. The set of criteria in front of you precisely describes the requirements. Once you have this agreement, move on to Stage 4.

▶ Stage 4 – Pre-Close

This stage is optional.

We use it when we want to gain some commitment from the customer before moving on to the matching part of the presentation, or to check that the customer is serious and not a time waster.

The pre-close is a conditional close. We ask if we can meet the requirements, whether we will win the order? You say: 'If we are able to meet each of these requirements to your satisfaction, will you feel comfortable proceeding with this?' The operative word is *if*.

The pre-close is a perfectly reasonable question to ask. You have spent time helping the customer to establish the criteria for ordering and you have confirmed that these represent all the requirements. So if you can now show how your product or service meets each requirement, the customer should be happy to proceed.

You assume that the customer will answer 'yes' to the pre-close. After all, they have just told you what the successful supplier will have done to win the order, so if you meet the criteria better than anybody else, of course they will go ahead with you.

So why could it be that after all your efforts, some customers still say, 'It depends.' You have agreed and confirmed the decision criteria, so what can it depend on if you meet all of the criteria better than anybody else?

'It depends' for one of the following reasons:

- They are not the decision maker.
- They do not feel comfortable with you or trust you fully because the relationship has not yet been built.
- They need to ratify the decision with somebody.
- They are unsure about the list.
- They suspect that a colleague may try to influence the decision.

When this happens, you have no choice but to go back through the sequence. Check the decision criteria, check the decision process and who is involved. Send in the draft specification and visit again. Whatever the reason, it must be uncovered before proceeding.

If you are unable to pre-close, it goes without saying that there is a good chance you are wasting your time. The general maxim here is, if you can't pre-close get out and come back later, or consider going higher/establishing another contact.

If you can pre-close – and a significant proportion of times you will – you move on to Stage 5.

▶ Stage 5 – Order of Importance

Like the pre-close, this stage is also optional.

If, when establishing the criteria for ordering in Stage 2, there are one or two vital requirements that you know you can match superbly, it is useful to highlight them now. This is when you use the 'Order of Importance'.

You are not concerned here with accurately ranking all the criteria. You want to highlight the one or two more important ones to which you know you have a good match. Put 1 alongside the most important. Put 2 alongside the second most important.

Ask the customer, 'Can you help me please? Which are the most important criteria? Can we prioritise these?'

Alternatively, it may be obvious from the customer's comments which is the main criteria. In this case you say, 'I think we've agreed that this is your most important point, so let's put 1 alongside that.'

▶ Stage 6 – Match and Tick

This is the presentation itself. You now show the customer how your product or service **matches** each requirement. Be enthusiastic, passionate and believable as you unfold what you have to offer.

Because LACPOMAC® is used with a written list of criteria, it allows you to tick off each requirement in turn during the matching stage and so verify that the customer is satisfied with your proposal.

At the end of the matching stage, **all the requirements should be ticked**. If you can't get a tick alongside one of them, the criteria for ordering stage was not completed correctly. Keep in mind also that all possible mismatches/objections should be pre-handled during Stage 2. You should have a set of criteria that you know you can match *before* the presentation begins.

When match and tick is complete, you can move on to Stage 7.

▶ Stage 7 – Ask Back

Here you double check that the customer is satisfied you can meet the requirements. This conveys your intense customer focus and helps build the relationship.

You ask, 'Are you happy that we've covered each of these points?' They are all ticked in front of the customer, so he says 'Yes'. This double checks that the matching stage is complete.

Once again, it's reassuring to know precisely where you are in the sale. At this penultimate stage in the LACPOMAC® process, you confirm that you have met all of the criteria.

It is important to satisfy the customer and yourself that you have met every criteria, if possible better than any other supplier. All relevant benefits, added value and distinctive competence must have been revealed by this stage.

▶ Stage 8 – Close

With LACPOMAC®, closing is very straightforward, in fact it is an automatic part of the process. Submit your proposal and ask for the business. A written proposal followed by a meeting is best. This is a good time to express how important the customer is and how much you want their business.

It is helpful if you can save something to delight the customer, like dedicated service levels or some extra item that may not add extra value but shows you really care.

And whether you win or lose, it is always worth holding a debrief to learn lessons for next time.

▶ The Selling Sequence
Summary of Main Points

The LACPOMAC® sequence provides a navigational tool, an underlying system of questions to move the sale forward. It isn't a holy grail or rocket science, but it is a straightforward eight-stage sequence that keeps you on track as the sale unfolds. When you know exactly where you are and where you are going, you develop that sureness of touch that invariably translates into more business.

The technique involves the following eight steps:

1. **Lead** into the sale. Warm the customer up with an opening benefit or credentials statement.
2. **Ask** about the buying criteria. This is the vital find out or fact find stage. The objective is to understand, define and shape the customer's requirements.
3. **Confirm** that the list of requirements is complete and that you have reached the end of the find out stage.
4. **Pre-close.** 'If we are able to meet each of these requirements to your satisfaction, will you feel comfortable proceeding with this?'
5. **Order of importance.** Highlight the most important criteria.
6. **Match.** Provide the appropriate solution. Match the benefits of your product or service to each requirement and tick off each one in turn.
7. **Ask back.** Double check that the customer is satisfied you can meet each requirement – 'Are you happy that we've covered each of these points?'
8. **Close.** Ask for the business.

Part Four
PERSONAL SKILLS

11
Develop the Right Stuff

Catapult yourself into the top echelon of achievers.

On a balmy Friday afternoon in May 1998, two of the wealthiest business people on the planet, Bill Gates, CEO of Microsoft, and Warren Buffet, Chairman of investment house Berkshire Hathaway, ran a seminar for 350 business school students at the University of Washington.

It is rare for seminar leaders to have a combined worth of $84 million, never mind the $84 billion of these two, so the audience was riveted in anticipation.

'How did you do it?', someone asked.

'It's not IQ, I'm sure you'll be glad to hear,' said Buffet. 'The big thing is output. IQ and talent represent the horsepower of the motor. Many people have a 400 horsepower motor, but only get 100 horsepower of output. It's way better to have a 200 horsepower motor and get all 200 horsepower of output.

People do things which interfere with the output they should get. It's about habits and character and temperament. Everyone can make it, some of you will and some of you won't. For the ones who won't, it will be because you get in your own way, not because the world won't allow you.'

He then described one of the most useful self-improvement tips I have ever encountered.

'I have one little suggestion for you. Pick out the person you admire most, and then write down why you admire them. Don't include yourself in this!

Then pick out the person that frankly you can stand the least and write down the qualities that turn you off in that person.

Look at what you admire and make up your mind to make those traits your own habits, and look at what you find really reprehensible in others and decide those are things you are not going to do. If you do that you'll find that you convert all of your horsepower into output.'

▶ Take Yourself to the Top

That wisdom sets the stage for this chapter and our investigation into the inner game of personal achievement.

I passionately believe that the ability to convince ourselves of our potential is the greatest selling skill of all. It's what personal leadership is all about. To win more business with this approach, one of the questions you must ask yourself is: 'Am I a two- or three-dimensional salesperson?'

The classic approach to sales training is two-dimensional. It focuses on product knowledge and skills training:

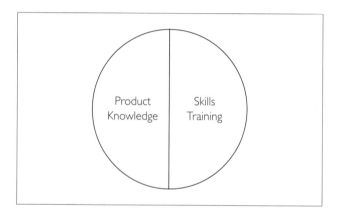

Many people take the view that if you give salespeople superb training in the products they sell and in modern professional selling skills – building relationships, using questions to uncover require-ments, matching the correct solution, selling against competition, closing, follow-up, writing proposals, negotiating – that's enough to prepare them to do an outstanding job. But it's not.

There are thousands of salespeople whose product knowledge is outstanding, whose understanding of sales skills and networking is superb, but whose results are still no more than average. They have neglected the third dimension, *personal development* – **you** as an individual, how you think, your drive, confidence, stamina, attitude, persistence and self-motivation.

Think of the most successful person you have ever met, in any field. What makes them that successful? What is the X factor that sets them apart? I'll bet it's not their knowledge or their expertise – it's their drive, their enthusiasm, their confidence. They have a mental toughness, an inner steel, a 'go for it' mentality. They think like a winner and when things don't go according to plan they know how to turn on sufficient energy and motivation to put themselves back on track.

To get to the top in sales you must have a willingness not only to work on your product knowledge and sales skills, but on yourself.

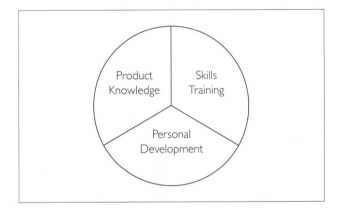

▶ Attitude Counts

The biggest single cause of failure in competitive selling is not lack of product knowledge, nor is it lack of sales skills – it's our personality under pressure. Top sellers have mental toughness and they work on it constantly. As motivational guru Zig Zigler taught, *it's your attitude not your aptitude that determines your altitude.*

Selling can be a cruel profession; like sport it has its highs and its lows. When things are going well it's the greatest job in the world – we love the feel of winning. But what happens when things don't click for us or we hit a dry spell. It's easy to lose confidence and begin a downward spiral. We get negative and start blaming others. As our sales figures lose their lustre, everything else seems to sink as well.

We have to be able to handle our yo-yo emotions. We have to stay strong. Mastery of this is critical to ensure that we are not a transient guest at the top table of selling. What really matters is how we run our mind.

Professional athletes take incredible care of their minds. Why should it be any different for us?

▶ Be Determined

Let people sense your strong will to succeed. We communicate with our words, our appearance, our manners, but especially with our sense of purpose. *Certainty is more persuasive than charm.* In business as in sport, the person who wins is usually the one who wants it the most.

Your fortunes rise and fall with your determination. Think of a sale that's coming up and ask yourself: 'How badly do I want it?'

> Socrates was approached by a student who said, 'I want more knowledge.'
> 'Knowledge is freely available if you look for it,' replied Socrates.
> 'I've tried that, but I still want more,' retorted the student.
> Sensing his mood, Socrates said, 'If you really want more, come with me.' He led the student down to the beach and walked across the sand into the water. When they were chest high, the well-built Socrates grabbed the student by the shoulders in a vice-like grip and held him under the water.
> The student kicked and twisted and fought, but still Socrates maintained his grip. Finally he allowed the student up.
> 'When you were under the water what did you want more than anything else?' asked Socrates.
> 'I wanted air, air, air,' gasped the student.
> 'When you want knowledge with the same intensity as you wanted that air, you will find all the knowledge you want.'

One of the questions I often ask at seminars is, 'How many of you believe you could run a marathon?' Usually, in a packed conference hall, five or six hands go up.

Then I ask, 'If I gave you £250,000 to run a marathon, how many of you believe you could do it?' Every hand goes up! And they'd do it, too.

What's changed? There is no way their ability to run a marathon has changed in maybe 30 seconds. What's changed is their *desire.*

You may be thinking, 'You made the pot sweet enough.' But that's not the point. It's the realisation that it's our desire not our ability that is so exciting. The desire comes first and you get the ability as you go along.

As a new salesperson I found selling difficult. I wasn't sure whether I had what it takes. The first few months of my sales career were a real struggle.

Then a colleague persuaded me to attend a personal development seminar. There I learned one of the great laws of achievement: it's desire, not ability, that counts.

It was as if someone had switched on a light inside me. I felt really motivated, because I had always thought ability was all important.

I'm a great fan of Madonna – not for her singing, although I enjoy that immensely, but for her determination. With annual gross sales of over $1 billion, you can't ignore the success of the material girl. *The Guinness Book of Hit Singles* describes Madonna as the most successful female pop artist of all time.

Madonna has said that at auditions there have often been others who can sing better than she can, act better, dance better – but no one wants the role as much as she does. Those who want something the most usually win.

To get the part of Eva Peron in *Evita*, Madonna wrote an eight-page letter to director Alan Parker saying how much she wanted the role. Keep in mind that she was already a megastar and you have an insight into her drive and focus.

She wrote in her diary at the time, 'When you want something badly enough it seems as if the whole earth conspires to help you get it.'

▶ Be Goal Oriented

The main source of determination is having a goal.

Imagine you're on a bicycle and the wheels aren't turning. What's about to happen? No catch questions here – you fall off. But the moment you start cycling towards somewhere your balance is restored.

Your career is similar to the bicycle. If you're simply doing a job but not going anywhere, determination and motivation disappear. However, as soon as you have a goal, a target that you really want to achieve, motivation is restored.

What is your goal? What do you want to achieve in the next three months? In the next 12 months? Nail it down.

You have to have a goal, a personal mission, a vision of the future that gives you the energy to pull through tough times. Then all you need to do when determination ebbs is to focus on your goal. Like a laser, a goal must be focused, aimed and *used*.

If you want real determination then get a BHAG – a Big Hairy Audacious Goal. Big goals are exciting. If you meet someone with no energy, no drive, it usually means that they have no goals or that the ones they do have have become boring. They need something new to aim for, something big, something exciting to fire up their drive and energy system.

Robert Schuller, who created the concept of *Possibility Thinking*, came up with one of the most exciting goal-deciding questions ever devised: *Imagine you couldn't fail, what one great thing would you dare to achieve?* Think about it, picture a success genie who grants you one wish, one goal which, once you decide on, will happen. What would it be?

Whatever your age, background and circumstances, I urge you to set your goals – and to do it now.

The explorer Robert Swan, the first man to walk unsupported to both North and South Poles, said, 'I've never seen the second hand on my watch going backwards yet. The most important thing is to live until you die, rather than exist until you die. Anything is possible if you put your mind to it.'

▶ Do What You Love

Does Celine Dion love to sing? Does Steve Redgrave love to row? Does Jacques Villeneuve love to drive? Does Stella McCartney love designing clothes?

We all do best what we love the most. The simple but profound key to loving what you do is to *do what you love.*

What three things do you enjoy most about your job? What makes you tingle with excitement? What makes you feel good about yourself? What gives you a faster heartbeat?

These are your values, what motivates you and keeps you high on life. Set goals and stretch yourself in these areas. They will lead you to your area of excellence.

Your goals and your values must fit with each other otherwise you will burn out. When setting a goal you must first decide what you enjoy and then increase your enjoyment of doing it. That keeps you motivated and gives you the energy to persevere no matter what comes along.

If you don't do what you enjoy, you'll feel caught up in a rat race and, as Lily Tomlin put it, 'The trouble with being in a rat race is even if you win, you're still a rat.'

▶ Find a Coach

Everyone needs a coach, someone who gives them a push from time to time. Most people achieve more if they are encouraged, motivated and coached, than if they try to go it alone. Get yourself a coach, someone who believes in you, who will stretch you and challenge you to set high goals.

Boxer Muhammad Ali was once asked to describe the greatest lesson he had learned in life. He recalled a fight against Sonny Liston for the heavyweight title in 1964: 'Liston was the strongest man I've ever fought. Every time I hit him, it hurt me more than it did him. I gave him everything I had. By the end of the sixth round I was completely spent. I couldn't even raise my arms. I couldn't even stand up.'

'I'm goin' home,' he told his trainer Angelo Dundee. 'I'm not going back in there. Throw in the towel.'

Dundee demanded that Ali get back in the ring. But the fighter refused. The bell rang and still Ali stayed put. Dundee pushed him and yelled, 'Get back in there and don't come out until you are heavyweight champion of the world.'

Ali struggled to his feet. Liston didn't. Ali won the title.

The experience taught him the importance of coaching: 'The greatest lesson I've learned is to have someone pushin' you and makin' you do things you don't think you can do.'

▶ Be Willing to Prepare Thoroughly

It's often said that many people have the will to win, but they don't all have the will to prepare.

Helen Sharman was working for Mars Confectionery. Driving home one night she heard on the car radio 'Astronaut wanted – no experience necessary'. An organisation had been set up to send the first Briton into space. Two people were needed to train as cosmonauts in Star City in Russia. After 18 months, one person would be launched into space to do experiments aboard the MIR space station.

'Go for it,' Helen thought and with thousands of others she applied for the job. There was a stringent selection process and Helen and one other were picked as trainee astronauts.

What a challenge. First she had to learn Russian, then they trained and trained and trained for every eventuality: emergency training, weightless training, simulator training, technical training.

On 18 May 1991 she and two crew mates were launched aboard a Soyuz capsule. After achieving orbit they faced a series of malfunctions. Inexplicably they lost control of the spacecraft's orientation and encountered difficulties with their life support, temperature and oxygen systems. To further compound the situation, they lost communication with earth. They had trained for thousands of hours confronting every possibility, but no one had foreseen all these malfunctions occurring at the same time. None of their previous training was helpful. The cosmonauts had to carry out remedial work they had never contemplated.

At a recent conference Helen said, 'We trained for all the things we had foreseen, but the real value was in the training that enabled you to deal with what you could not foresee – training in how to think, how to cope with the unexpected.'

There is no way we can ever prepare for every situation we encounter, but if we develop the right approach, if we train ourselves to think constructively and confidently, we're halfway there.

▶ Decide to Be A Top Performer

Many people start a new job or their job description changes and they have the attitude, 'I'll wait and see whether or not this job comes up to my expectations.' It never will.

The job couldn't care less. It's unimportant when we get into the business: what matters is when the business gets into us.

Decide to be a top performer. Right now, reinforce your decision to be a top producer in your field.

Unsuccessful people flit from job to job. They wend their way through life never deciding to master anything in particular. Their attitude is 'I'm waiting to be discovered', but they never are.

I began my working life as an electronics engineer working in the aerospace industry. There I spoke to colleagues who were two or three years ahead of me, only to find they were short of money and somewhat disillusioned. I wanted to get ahead, so I changed companies and moved into an export role. After a while that too lost its appeal, so I moved again, this time to a computer company as a systems analyst. Job to job to job, nothing seemed to click for me.

I often used the phrase 'I'm searching for my niche.' Finally I moved into sales and after a wobbly start attended the seminar mentioned earlier. One of the speakers, an ebullient Australian, hammered into us: 'You don't discover your greatest potential, you decide on it and then go to work on yourself to develop the necessary skills and attributes.'

I was hooked and have been an advocate of personal development training ever since.

▶ Energy Sells

How we say things is often more important than what we say. Communication and energy cannot be separated. Communication is an inside-out process. When you attend one of our courses, in front of you is a tent card. Your name is on the side facing the trainer and facing you is the phrase, 'Nothing great was ever achieved without enthusiasm.'

People enjoy doing business with enthusiastic, energetic people. We are not talking about an over-the-top exuberance, but the enthusiasm that comes from a belief and conviction in the value of what we do. That enthusiasm is the highest-paid quality on earth.

I will never forget reading an article about Andrew Carnegie. At the time of the Industrial Revolution he was one of the world's wealthiest men, the Bill Gates of his era. He once gave one of his staff a million-dollar annual bonus, a staggering amount for the time. When a reporter asked him why, Carnegie replied, 'Because he has the ability to excite people. I'll pay more for that trait than for any other.'

It exasperates me when organisations spend so much on advertising and then throw it away by not hiring good people and training them how to optimise the interest generated. I suppose they think such things a waste of money. Low-energy people communicate a loser's attitude. If they are uninspired by their products and services, why should the customer be otherwise?

> Listening to the radio at home one Sunday morning, I heard an appeal. 'Donate £12 and help an old lady to see,' said Judi Dench, the narrator.
> I was moved and thought what a brilliant, fabulous appeal. Eager to contribute, I picked up the phone, credit card to hand. The telesales person who answered had one of the flattest, most disinterested, unenthusiastic, mechanical, boring tones I have encountered. She deflated my enthusiasm in an instant. I did contribute, but if she had reciprocated my enthusiasm she could so easily have increased my donation – and turned me into a regular contributor. This lady let her organisation down.
> Contrast that with the Holiday Inn in Paris. I called to order room service and was greeted with an energetic, bright, fresh 'Mr Fielder, Good morning.' Although that happened eight years ago, I was so impressed I've been telling the story ever since. And whenever I'm in Paris, that's where I stay.

When you are selling, people will agree to buy based more on your conviction and enthusiasm than on your excellent product knowledge.

Energy reflects a passion, an enjoyment for what you do. People feel confident recommending you to others. '*Energy sells*' – write that on a card and tape it where you'll see it several times a day.

▶ Presentation Skills

If there is one skill worth mastering, it is being an effective presenter and speaker. Nothing, but nothing, will build your confidence more effectively.

Most people think that presentation training is just about overcoming the stark terror of standing up in front of a group, but the confidence boost that comes from learning to sell to a group carries across to the face-to-face sale.

Presentation training can indeed be a demanding, white knuckle experience, but training that doesn't stretch us, that doesn't help us to perform when we're on the line, is of limited value. When you stretch people, they grow.

The discipline of preparation, of thinking through the audience's requirements and expectations, of connecting with people personally, of establishing trust, is what provides a real insight into what selling is really about.

Whatever level of presentation skill you have now, my strongest advice to you is develop it further. Even people whose knees knock and hands shake before the smallest group can learn how to speak well.

It's easier than it looks, much easier. You just have to work at it, polish it and do it over and over. Take every opportunity to stand up and present your ideas.

No skill opens more doors, creates more visibility or motivates more effectively.

▶ Develop the Right Stuff
Summary of Main Points

Important skills for salespeople to develop include the following:

- **Be determined.** Certainty is more persuasive than charm. Those who want it the most usually win. The main source of determination is having a goal, something exciting to aim for, something that stirs the blood.
- **Decide to be outstanding.** You don't discover your greatest potential, you decide on it. Right now reinforce your decision to be outstanding in your field.

- **Energy sells**. Communication and energy cannot be separated. Communication is an inside-out process. Enthusiasm is a universal language, one that everyone recognises.
- **Learning to speak in public** will build your confidence and self-esteem more effectively than anything else you can learn. This confidence carries across to the face-to-face sale.

12
Develop Success Mental Health

Tough times don't last – but tough people do.

Some years ago I attended a large national sales conference. Before it began, I was chatting to guests when in walked George, an account manager I hadn't seen for several months. I walked up and said hello.

'Hi, Robin,' he replied.

Then I made a mistake and asked, 'How is everything?' It took him about 15 minutes to explain.

'Robin, things are really tough at the moment, nothing is going according to plan. I've got problems on problems. Even my problems have got problems.' He was appallingly negative. 'You know these people getting Top Producer Awards today, well I'm sure I could be up there if I didn't have these problems – problems seem to have held me back all of my life.'

He went on, 'If only there was some way I could get rid of them, you'd see what I would achieve.'

'George, maybe I've got some help for you – I know a place where there are 78,000 people who have found a way to exist without any problems. In fact, I spoke to the general manager there and he told me that not one of them had a single problem. No big problems, no small problems, no problems at all.'

George's face lit up like a roman candle. 'Tell me where it is.'

'I'll tell you, George, but I don't think it's quite what you had in mind. It's Hendon Cemetery in North West London.'

This story may be amusing but it has a serious side. The only people who are problem free are no longer with us, therefore problems constitute a sign of life! The more problems we have, the more alive we are. Whoever said 'Problems and progress go together, you can't have one without the other' had it about right.

This approach to adversity represents what could be called *success* mental health. It is about how we handle the setbacks we encounter. Many people are physically healthy, but they may not be mentally healthy in their attitude to life.

The secret is not to be problem free; that's an unattainable illusion. It's to have a positive, energetic approach to solving our problems.

▶ How to Handle Adversity

A famous actress once remarked, 'It's not whether you get knocked down, it's whether you get up.' Every individual has odds to battle and difficulties to surmount. Those who win through have the knack of facing adversity without losing their drive and energy. Mental strength is hard to define, but it's in those who struggle towards their goals with guts and panache.

Here are four rules to help in the development of success mental health.

It's a challenge, not a problem

Stop using the word 'problem'. It's a depressing, negative anchor. Instead use 'challenge': 'We've got some terrific challenges – let's solve them. Let's turn them to our advantage and let's do it now.'

Challenge is a positive, energy-enhancing word that is much more likely to inspire us to find a solution. It's half full rather than half empty, 'X is a challenge for me' rather than 'X is a problem for me'.

There is no failure, only feedback

When a guided missile is off course, feedback sensors detect the error and correct the trajectory. It is awareness of the error that enables the missile to achieve its accuracy.

Have the same attitude towards yourself. When you make a mistake, it's not a failure, it's simply feedback that your goal-seeking mechanism requires to get you back on track.

Computer programmers know that the first time they run a new program it probably won't run correctly. They have to debug it. They don't get upset or feel they have failed – they make corrections and alter course based on what they've learned.

The best thing you can do with a mistake is to accept it as a learning experience. Whenever something goes awry, stay strong and say to yourself, 'That's interesting feedback, how can I learn from this, how can I turn this to my advantage?' But don't dwell on what has happened.

Energetic, positive people are gutted by adversity just as much as everyone else. The difference is what happens next.

Be keenly aware of how you react to adversity. When you catch yourself responding weakly, slam the palm of your hand on your desk, your knee, your steering wheel or whatever and shout 'Stop! Delete!' – and refocus on the picture of your desired outcome.

A positive mindset is your most valued possession.

Turn it to your advantage

Positive people see opportunity in adversity. Negative people think the grass is brown on both sides of the fence. Napoleon Hill, in his book *Think and Grow Rich*, puts it this way: 'Every adversity carries with it the seed of an equivalent or greater benefit.'

If your car is stolen while you're out visiting a customer, do you get annoyed, kick the kerb and fume, or do you sit down calmly and think about what car you'd like next?

> There was a woman who cycled competitively. She was good, but whenever she was passed during a race, she couldn't come back. She invariably lost. Her coach taught her to turn this to her advantage. Now when another cyclist passes her she says, 'Here's my opportunity to let her pull me along and take the strain of being the lead cyclist.' She then waits for the opportunity to strike back and beat the other competitor to the finish.

A solution does exist – all you have to do is find it

The world may be full of problems, but it's also full of solutions. Realising this gets our creative juices flowing, it turns on our creativity. The moment we say, 'This is difficult, this is not going to work, this is going to be tough', we turn our creativity off.

Keep your mind focused on the solution. Visualise what life will be like with the challenge solved.

▶ Build Self-Confidence

You have within you the resources you need to achieve what you want – you just have to believe it. As lateral thinking specialist Edward de Bono said, 'You're a genius, the only trouble is you don't realise it.'

Consider this: in front of you is a 20-foot wooden plank resting on the floor. Can you picture yourself walking along it? Easy.

Now imagine the same plank of wood suspended between two supports 100 feet in the air. What do you picture now when you think of walking along it? Unless you are a circus performer, you see yourself falling. Your fears are real because the mind completes the picture.

Positive or negative, the mind completes whatever picture we put into it – so learn to use positive pictures. This is the power of mental rehearsal or visualisation to build confidence. You can use it for any kind of performance preparation. Visualisation is routine training in the sports world, but it works just as well in business.

> Andrea Nierenberg knew the sale was a long shot. Her training and communications company usually worked with small and mid-size firms. This was a huge company that she was trying to land as a client. What if they thought she was out of her league?
> The week before the presentation, she started priming herself. Each day, on waking and when she went to bed, she closed her eyes and relaxed. She pictured a movie screen. There on the screen, larger than life, she watched herself confidently reaching an agreement with the client. When the critical day came, that's exactly what happened. It was as if her mind knew what to do – she'd been here before.

It's fascinating how our language reveals the visual nature of our thoughts. We talk about foresight, hindsight, insight, future scenarios, perspective, points of view, supervision, intuition (from the Latin 'to look at'). The mind programs itself through pictures.

French psychologist Emile Coué discovered that when the words and the pictures we use pull in opposite directions, the pictures always dominate. This led him to his famous law: when the will and the imagination are in conflict, the imagination always wins.

The point is, if we've been telling ourselves 'I'm a great sales-person', 'I'm a good manager', 'I'm a great communicator', 'I'm a winner', but seeing the opposite – the opposite is what we get.

▶ Focus on the Outcome

Focus is a quick form of mental preparation. To use it, simply lock your mind on to the picture of the outcome you want. Call it up like a CD-ROM image.

Do it before you give a business presentation, before you pick up the phone, before you meet a customer, before you attend a social event, before you write a proposal, before you chair a meeting, before an interview or counselling session. Learn to lock your mind on the desired outcome. Imagine that you are one minute after the successful completion of whatever it is you want to achieve. How do you feel? What do you see?

The more powerful the mental rehearsal, the greater the confidence you will experience.

> Lucy was an experienced and successful trainer for a fast-growing management consultancy, but she always felt nervous before talking to a group. Her organisation asked her to address the national conference. She was terrified and her nerves were a real jangle. She planned and rehearsed over and over what she wanted to say and was convinced it was perfect for the audience, but she was distressed by the thought that her nerves would ruin her performance on the day.
> Her manager told her to visualise the desired outcome. Hold a picture of the audience applauding, of people coming up afterwards and congratulating you. Picture yourself relaxed and on your best form.
> It worked. She got great reviews and really enjoyed it. She is now highly sought after as a conference speaker, work that she enjoys more than almost anything else she does.

Visualisation is like filing a flight plan. Having the right expectations, the right picture of what you want to achieve before you start the journey, is essential if you are going to reach the planned destination on schedule.

Whatever you want to achieve, see it now. Think about it every day. Make sure it's the first thing on your mind when you wake up and the last thought you have at night when you go to sleep.

▶ Manufacture Confidence Physically

Visualisation is how you mentally build your confidence, but you can also build it physically. One of the most effective techniques you can learn is centring.

Centring is an ancient personal development skill devised some 2,000 years ago by Tibetan monks. It is a technique that primarily uses breathing to help us regain our composure and think clearly in the midst of a great deal of energy.

Research shows you cannot experience nervousness unless you are breathing as if you are nervous. If you feel tense, nervous, fearful, anxious or self-conscious before an important event or meeting, your arousal level is too high. You're not really in control. These feelings are the opposite of being centred.

People say take a deep breath, but they don't tell you how. Through bio-feedback it has been found that when you inhale, muscle tension throughout the body increases; when you hold your breath it stays the same. But when you exhale, muscle tension reduces. So to regain your composure and relax, which should be longer, the in breath or the out breath? The answer, of course, is the out breath.

Here's how to take a centring breath:

- Inhale to a count of four (ideally, but not necessarily, through your nose).
- Hold your breath briefly.
- Breath out *slowly* to a count of 10 through your mouth.

The slow out breath relaxes you. As you breathe out, hold your hand two or three inches in front of your mouth and softly blow into it. You'll feel the gentle pressure and so become more aware of the slowing-down effect.

When you are very nervous, three or four of these slow out breaths will bring your arousal level back to normal.

▶ 'I Can Handle It'

'I can handle it' is one of the most inspiring phrases you can ever use. The four words provide strength and personal power over how you react to events. They drown out the inner voice of doom and gloom. Use them whenever anything new or demanding appears:

- 'What if we grow too quickly?' – 'I can handle it.'
- 'This new IT system is a challenge.' – 'I can handle it.'
- 'What if Mary leaves?' – 'I can handle it.'
- 'There's a lot to learn.' – 'I can handle it.'
- 'This is a *big* project.' – 'I can handle it.'

'I can handle it' is incredibly effective. It speaks to a *can do* mentality and reinforces our ability to influence events. Best of all, it makes us feel in control of what's going on around us. If we're in control we feel positive, energised and resourceful. If we're not, we feel powerless, listless and negative. We lack resourcefulness.

Companies can only change when people do and 'I can handle it' is brilliant for self-empowerment. Spend a few moments thinking about how you can use it in your own life. As Jack Welch of GE famously said, 'Control your destiny or someone else will.'

If you're a manager or team leader, install the same thought process into your team. Whenever difficulties or potential conflicts arise, have the attitude: 'We can handle it.'

▶ Be Persistent

There is one mistake you must never make – you must never, ever quit. How many quitters do you know who are successful? Probably none. Achievers hang in there, no matter what.

If right now you are experiencing difficult times, perhaps you are feeling drained overcoming one challenge after another, perhaps you are frustrated by events that cause you to take two steps backward for each step forward. I urge you to persevere. You are not alone:

- Michael Jordan was dropped from his school basketball team.
- Nigel Mansell had retired once before he won the Formula 1 World Championship.
- Steven Spielberg couldn't get into film school.
- Both Henry Ford and Walt Disney went bankrupt early in their careers.
- Chuck Jaeger, who became the first person to break the sound barrier, threw up on his first flight as a passenger. He vowed never to go back up again.
- Thomas Edison was thrown out of school in the early grades when the teachers decided he couldn't do the work.
- Bob Dylan was booed off stage at a high school talent show.
- Roger Bannister was told that the four-minute mile was impossible.
- Nelson Mandela hung on to his goal despite years of imprisonment.
- Michael Blake, author of *Dances with Wolves*, wrote more than 20 screenplays and had nothing but rejections for 25 years.

▶ 'How Can I Do It Better?'

Think progress. Believe in progress. Push for progress. You may be one of the top salespeople or managers in your company, but the day someone in that position says 'It's great, let's leave it alone', they are sliding backwards. Your thought process should be, 'I'm doing well, but how can I do it better?'

As well as 'How can I do it better?', let's also think 'How can I do *more*?' Capacity is a state of mind. We all think we're doing as much as we can until we meet someone who is doing more.

> I recall in my early career being part of a terrific sales team in a financial services business. I was really short of money and was working like crazy to sort things out. Some days I would make 11 or 12 presentations and I thought that was absolutely the most anyone could make.
> Then I was introduced to Ray Hampton – he was making 15 presentations a day. I was stunned and suddenly realised I was fiddling about and needed to get my act together. We can always do more.

The brilliant nineteenth-century psychologist William James said it best: 'If you keep faithfully busy you can with perfect certainty count on waking up some fine morning to find yourself one of the competent ones of your generation in whatever pursuit you have singled out.'

▶ Be a Learner

Recognise the rising shift to self-reliance. Jobs for life are no more. And as educator Lewis Perelman put it, 'Learning is what most adults will do for a living in the 21st century.' The future is in our hands and we are responsible – that's the good news and the bad news. The good news is that we are in control of our own destiny; the bad news is that there are no excuses.

To succeed in this fast new world of personal development we must take 100 per cent responsibility for our future. We must continually learn new ways of getting the best out of ourselves, master new skills and, importantly, make sure that our personal goals and those of the organisation we work with match up. It's the only way to sustain energy and drive.

Consider a company called YOU plc. You are the CEO, sales director, production director, marketing director and financial director of this organisation. If you were an outside investor, would you invest in it? To be convinced you'd want to know that YOU plc was planning for the future, embracing the latest technology and excited about the upcoming potential in its markets. You'd want to know it was investing in training and developing its key resources – in this case, you.

How do you stand against these requirements?

▶ Feed Your Mind with Positive Input

You find what you look for. If you look for opportunity, that's what you find. If you look for what's wrong, that's what you find. Have an abundance mentality, not a scarcity one. If you think there is plenty of business and profit for everyone, that's what you'll find. If you think there is too much competition and not enough business to go round, that's what you'll find too. Constant positive input equals constant positive output.

> Russell H. Conwell's classic *Acres of Diamonds* is the story of a farmer in Asia named Al Hafed, who heard about other farmers who made a fortune by discovering a diamond mine. These stories so excited this particular farmer that he could hardly wait to sell his farm and begin searching for his own mine. He sold up and then spent the rest of his life wandering first the Asian then the European continents unsuccessfully searching for his dreams. Finally one day, broke, frustrated, in a fit of despondency, he threw himself from a cliff into the sea and drowned.
>
> Meanwhile, the man who had bought the farm was walking through the property one day and he came across a large unusually shaped stone that later turned out to be a diamond of enormous value.
>
> They later discovered that the farm was covered with these stones. In fact it became one of the world's wealthiest diamond mines, the Golconda, from which came the great Kohinoor diamond that is part of the British crown jewels and the largest crown diamond on earth in the crown jewels of Russia.
>
> The first farmer had owned acres of diamonds but had sold them for virtually nothing in order to look for them elsewhere. If only he had taken the time to study, to learn what diamonds looked like in their raw state and then thoroughly explored the land he already owned, he would have discovered the wealth he sought.

▶ Eliminate the Negative

Keep away from negative, moaning, whinging, criticising, complaining people. They will drag you down to their level.

When people say such things as 'You can't do that', 'You'll never sell to him', 'You're a nice person but you're not cut out to get to the top', they damage our career and our confidence. They spew out their negative garbage and it's dangerous. Such nay-sayers can hold us back for months, sometimes years, because negativity is so powerful.

> The laws of aerodynamics tell us that the bumble bee cannot fly. Its wings are too small, it's too heavy, it has insufficient muscle and it's the

wrong shape. Technically there is no known way that a bumble bee can get off the ground. But fortunately, no one has told the bees and they carry on flying around.

Imagine you could communicate with one: 'Bumble bee, this is a printout of your flight geometry. According to this, you cannot fly. Your wings are too small, you've insufficient muscle and you're the wrong shape. There's no way you can make it.'

The bumble bee would be too frightened to attempt to fly. Here's the point: how many of us are too frightened even to attempt something because of what someone else once said we couldn't do?

Keep away from negative people. If you associate with negative, unpleasant or miserable people, then sooner or later you'll adopt the same behaviour, no matter how cheerful you were before spending time with them. Be fiercely aware of the corrosive effect of the drip, drip, drip input of half-empty thinkers.

Don't attempt to convert negative people to being positive, at least not by yourself. You've heard the expression: 'Don't fight with pigs, you both get covered in muck, but the pig likes it.' In this case the pig is the negativity.

Go to great lengths to protect your positive mindset. Declare your office a neg-free zone. Don't be subtle. Get a can of air freshener, wrap a new label around it with 'Neg Repellent' printed in large capitals and leave it on your desk. Next time anyone near you says anything negative, give them a squirt. They'll soon get the message!

Avoid reading tabloid exposes of other people's misfortunes and tragedies. Getting hooked on such stuff will make you jaded and cynical. Regard everything as half full rather than half empty. Make it a habit to start the day on a positive note.

In a chameleon-like way, we tend to take on the attitude of the people we spend most of our time with. So surround yourself with people who, when they see you encounter an obstacle, say, 'Hang in there, you can do it. We believe in you.' Don't let anyone tell you that what you want is impossible. If the people around you don't support you in achieving your goals, avoid them or, at the very least, spend less time with them.

And last but definitely not least, remember to be a positive, upbeat influence yourself. The four most powerful words you can say to a colleague, a family member, a friend, or a valued team player are 'I believe in you'. Be a source of strength to others. What you hand out, you get back, usually multiplied.

▶ Developing Success Mental Health Summary of Main Points

You may be physically healthy, but is your attitude to life mentally healthy? Do you have a positive, energetic approach to solving your challenges? How people handle adversity determines to a great extent who is successful and who isn't. Recognise that setbacks constitute a sign of life.

Four rules for handling adversity:

- Stop using the word problem; instead use the word challenge. Think 'x' is a challenge for me, rather than 'x' is a problem for me.
- There is no failure, only feedback. Don't beat yourself up when something goes awry. It's simply interesting feedback you can learn from. Be keenly aware of how you respond to adversity. Use 'Stop! Delete!' to keep your mind focused on the positive.
- When adversity strikes, ask yourself, 'How can I turn this to my advantage?'
- Realise that a solution does exist. All you have to do is find it.

Additional ways to develop success mental health:

- Build self-confidence. Winners see the act of winning in advance, they know that what you see is who you'll be. Use mental rehearsal: picture the desired outcome and lock your mind on it. Regain your composure and confidence in the middle of a great deal of energy by taking two or three centring breaths.
- Use 'I can handle it'. It makes you feel in control of what's going on around you.
- Become a 'How can I do it better?' person.
- Be a learner. The future belongs to those who prepare for it.
- Feed your mind with positive input. Constant positive input equals constant positive output. You find what you look for – if you look for opportunity, that's what you find. If you look for what's wrong, that's what you find.
- Eliminate the negative. Negative thinking *never* helps you. The most it can do is make you feel lousy and frustrated. Instead, spend time with proactive, optimistic, goal-oriented people.

A Final Word

The overriding message of this book is that we should rethink our approach to selling. The rules of engagement have changed because business is changing.

Selling in the twenty-first century is about building relationships, solving problems and consultation. It's about being *in* business with the customer, not *doing* business with them. It's about being a consultant and a partner. Competition has shifted from who has the best product to who can best improve the customer's operations.

The second message is that skills training is never enough – we must also develop the will to win. Winners don't give up, they get up! The greatest selling skill of all is the ability to convince ourselves of our potential.

To tie everything together, there are 12 fundamentals I would like to leave you with. You enhance your edge over your competition when:

1. You sell the difference. What are you known for? What's so special about your offering?
2. You always have the other person's interests at heart. What you hand out, you get back.
3. You adopt the attitude: 'I am not in selling, I am in problem solving.'
4. You bring more to the table than just a sale. You test this by asking yourself, 'Would my customer still hire me as a consultant if I no longer had my product or service to sell?'
5. You are polite, vibrantly enthusiastic and openly straightforward in communicating with *everyone*.
6. You master the art of listening someone into a sale.
7. You build credibility by nurturing your reputation and having testimonial evidence to support your claims.

8. You cover the bases by talking to everyone in the account who will be affected by your proposal.
9. You are passionate about implementation. The sale begins the sale for the customer.
10. You love what you do and constantly work at doing it better.
11. You are a positive role model for those around you.
12. You master the temptation to quit. Perseverance is the big secret used by the world's highest achievers to propel themselves to stunning success.

Appendix I
Making the Appointment

Suggested approach and script.

This appendix will help you if you need some assistance with making appointments. Let's start by reviewing the initial telephone contact.

You have a lead. How do you get through to the decision maker or key influencer and make the appointment? No matter how you sourced the lead, it pays to plan the call, not just to have a stab at it.

You have a small time window of opportunity. At the end of the call the customer will either agree to take it further or put the phone down.

Obviously it's best if you have a name of the person to talk to. If you don't, ask the switchboard who is in charge of or responsible for, say, sales training. Establish the name of your customer, including his or her first name. Not Mr Davidson, but John Davidson.

If the receptionist on the switchboard says 'I don't know' or 'I'm new here', ask to be put through to the sales department or to customer service. Whatever you sell, they are usually helpful and courteous and will guide you in the right direction.

Once you're through, if the person asks 'What's it regarding?', make sure your response is a benefit to the prospective purchaser.

On most occasions, the PA will take your call. I know I'm not being politically correct here, but there are still more female than male PAs. *You must sound interesting to her.* Nowadays secretaries are more and more executive assistants. Their job is to screen their busy boss, to keep out inappropriate calls and let in appropriate ones. You have to sell the assistant on why you should be put through. Any seller who thinks the way to get through is to sound important has it badly wrong. Yet you would be amazed how many salespeople still treat secretaries as educationally subnormal irritations to their job. Incredulously, some even put on the 'Do you know who I am?' act.

Whenever my PA puts a call through, I invariably ask her, 'What's he calling about?' I value her impressions. The only calls that never get put through are from those who refuse to explain anything to her and insist on talking to me direct. They live in yesterday's world. It's my PA's job to decide who and what are interesting.

Two tips are helpful here:

1. Make an ally of the PA. Ask for her help in the best way to present your case to her boss. This is always a good idea. Build rapport with everyone, not just the person you want to speak to. It really annoys me when salespeople treat support staff poorly. Be scrupulously polite.
2. Persist. Call several times, say twice a week for a month. She will finally say to her boss, 'Oh, you must call Robin Fielder, he must have called eight times. I don't know what to say to him anymore, do have a word with him'.

---

1. Check you are speaking to the right person. 'Is that Mr Davidson?'
2. Introduce yourself. Include your first name, don't call yourself Mr/Mrs/Miss.

   - 'Good morning. Thank you for taking my call. It's Robin Fielder here from LDL. We are a sales and management training consultancy.'

   If you feel so inclined add, 'This is a new business call, is now a good time to speak?' Nothing is more annoying than talking with a salesperson who has not make it clear why they are calling.

3. Open the conversation with a relevant comment that legitimises and gives a reason for your call. This is often called a 'peg'.

   - 'It's been a long time since we've been in contact.'
   - 'I noticed you have just won a large export order.'
   - 'We have a mutual friend in Frank Davis who suggested I contact you.'
   - 'We have recently concluded a training assignment for your Bristol office and the sales manager, Susan Evans, suggested I contact you.'
   - 'I wrote to you recently regarding our new training programme.'

■ 'We have been sending you monthly newsletters about our approach to training. Have you found these useful?'

4. Now use your Opening Hot Button Statement (OHBS).

As we saw in Chapter 4, this is a general 'What's in it for the customer' statement designed to spark interest and tempt him with some kind of benefit. It goes without saying that you must be able to prove any claim you make.

■ 'The reason I'm calling is we have done a lot of work in your industry and we've been able to assist a number of other organisations in your market sector to improve their sales revenue by up to 20 per cent using a new approach to sales training. At this stage I don't know whether we could do something similar for you, but I'd like to arrange a meeting to discuss it. How does that sound?'

In fact, as discussed in Chapter 5 it is usually better to ask some initial questions prior to requesting the appointment.

One of our clients is a high street bank. When we first started working with them they were using this telephone approach:
'Good morning, Mr Prospect, it's Fred Smith here from the XYZ Bank. The reason I'm calling you is we have just set up a financial planning service and we wondered whether you might like some financial advice on protection and pensions. Would you be interested in having a financial interview with one of our advisers?'
What do you reckon most people said?
'No, thank you.'
There is no benefit, it sounds flat. It also has some turn-off words like interview and financial planning. They changed it. After an introductory letter to the prospective customer from the branch manager, they rang and said:
'Good morning, Mr Prospect, it's Fred Smith here from the XYZ Bank. We have been able to assist a number of customers in a similar situation to yourself by providing them with a free review of their financial requirements. In many cases we were able to help these customers to save some tax. Now I don't know whether we can do the same for you, but what we would like to do is to arrange a meeting to discuss it. How does that sound?'
Thirty per cent of people said yes. The benefit is clearly the possibility of saving tax.

5. Close on the appointment.

Suggest a time, give the customer various choices.

You are encouraging the prospective customer to look in his diary. He may well give you a better time if appropriate.

6. Repeat the arrangement

'Fine, Mr Davidson, I'll look forward to seeing you at 2.15 on Tuesday 14 March.'

After you have made the appointment, drop the customer a line/or email confirming the arrangement.

Appendix II

Gaining Commitment and Closing

Don't just build the relationship, gain commitment.

Once you have established trust, reduced risk, clearly understood the customer's requirements and provided an appropriate solution, the business is yours, though, as we've seen, you must ask for it.

But what happens at the end of the presentation, or any important stage in a multi-visit sale, if there is still some mismatch on the mind of your customer?

She will hesitate over the proposals, usually with the courteous phrase, 'I want to think about it.'

You probably think, 'Oh no – here we go again.' After all your hard work in building the relationship, you are at the brink of the sale and it looks as if it's going to be thwarted by the buyer's natural instinct to hesitate at the moment of buying.

▶ What Do You Do?

What *can* you do to gain commitment at this crucial stage? The relationship-building school of selling tells us that if you have built a strong enough relationship, the business should take care of itself – but, as we discussed earlier, it's not always true. Someone once said, 'You've built a great relationship. Now what are you going to *do* with it?'

Having superb relationship and interpersonal skills is not enough. You must complement these skills with a *process* for gaining commitment. That is the function of the LACPAAC® model.

You can see I like acronyms. They make it easier to remember key points and the order in which they should be used.

A million miles from the old-style closing tactics, LACPAAC® is a consultative approach that will give you a real edge in the final stages of the sale. It works in all sales environments and has evolved into one of the most effective selling processes ever devised. You'll find the model provides you with a profound insight into the structure of gaining commitment.

As training providers, we've had people leave our courses and return to customers who the previous week had said said, 'I want to think about it.' They've visited them again, used LACPAAC® and won the business.

I've had major account salespeople telephone to tell me they've just tied up the biggest sale of their career, thanks to LACPAAC®. I recall one account director at a well-known advertising agency who told tell me how he'd used it to win a £1 million account that he'd been struggling with for months.

People have even written to say how they have managed to get themselves married using the process. That's got to be the ultimate relationship sale.

> Be careful to differentiate between LACPAAC® and LACPOMAC®. LACPAAC® is a model for handling mismatch at the end of the sales discussion. LACPOMAC® is a navigational tool for the entire sales process.

Here's how it works:

▶ Understanding LACPAAC®

Since 'I want to think about it' at the end of the sales discussion is indicative of residual mismatch, your objective is to establish which areas of mismatch currently exist and are preventing your customer from going ahead – in other words, which so-called objections are on her mind.

Assuming you are able to identify these areas, *then* satisfactorily match to them, the business will be closed, or you will have gained commitment to take it to the next stage.

LACPAAC® takes this concept and makes it both practical and easy to use. Not only does it provide a seven-step model for handling *mismatch* that still exists at the end of the presentation, it also reinforces the feeling of trust and further cements the relationship. That's its strength.

More than 200,000 salespeople have been trained in LACPAAC®. The seven-stage sequence is regarded as one of the most effective selling skills you can ever learn. Once you master it, never again will you build great relationships and leave empty handed, kicking yourself for not getting the business.

▶ The LACPAAC® Model

Five of the seven steps in the LACPAAC® model are questions. This reinforces the questions not reasons concept that we've talked about throughout the book.

LACPAAC® takes a series of highly effective stand-alone skills and concentrates them into a single sequence. In effect, it's a flow chart that optimises the order in which you use your available skills at the end of a sales discussion.

▶ Getting into LACPAAC®

Here's how you enter the process:

> Customer: 'I want to think about it.'
> Seller: 'I agree you should think about it, but usually when someone says that, it's because they are unsure of certain points. Is that the case for you?'
> Customer: 'Yes, there are some things that I'm not sure about.'

It is important that your first response to the customer's, '*I want to think about it*' is agreement. People buy people first and whatever else second. Put the phrase into your own words, but make sure you convey to the customer that you *understand* her desire to chew it over. Once this is achieved you move on to Stage 1 of LACPAAC®.

1. L stands for LIST

You now say: '*May I suggest we jot them down so we can both see what we're looking at?*'

Then on a clean pad of paper, list the numbers 1 to 6 down the left-hand side of the page. As you write, say the numbers quietly.

It's important to appreciate that to use LACPAAC® successfully, you don't have to list 1 to 6, you could go 1 to 4 or 1 to 8, it depends on the complexity of your proposal. However, most people find that listing 1 to 6 works well for them.

You now move to Stage 2.

2. A stands for ASK BACK

You ask: '*What points are you unsure of?*' She tells you and you jot them down on the list. As you do, keep these tips in mind. First, try to capture the mismatch (objection) in one word. If you have to go to two or three words that's fine, but avoid writing too much: keep it simple and short. Secondly, if your customer comes up with a mismatch that you are nervous about, don't show your concern. And thirdly, make no attempt to answer any of the points at this stage, unless they're very simple.

On completion of Stage 2, you will have a written list in front of you looking something like this:

1. Price
2. Competition
3. Delivery
4. Support
5.
6.

The mismatches shown here are obviously only for example. Your list will reflect the particular concerns of your customer.

3. C stands for CLOSE-IN

As the name implies, you are now going to draw the discussion to a focal point. The objective is to gain the customer's agreement that the list of concerns in front of you is complete. You say: '*Are those all the points you have?*'

In most cases the customer will say 'Yes'. You then draw a line under the list. In the unlikely event she says 'No,' don't be concerned, simply loop back to Phase 2 by asking, '*What other points do you have?*'

The objective is to continue asking back until you have agreement that all the points are noted. Once you have agreement, your list will look like this:

1. Price
2. Competition
3. Delivery
4. Support
_____
5.
6.

4. P stands for PRE-CLOSE

This is the pivotal stage in using LACPAAC®. Having carefully established the customer's mismatches with Stages 2 and 3 above, you now ask: '*If I am able to deal with each of these points to your satisfaction, will you then feel comfortable proceeding with this?*'

> The pre-close question is easily varied to suit the desired outcome of the conversation. For example, if the objective is to get the customer to recommend your services to her clients, then the pre-close becomes: '*If I am able to deal with each of these points to your complete satisfaction, will you recommend these services to your clients?*'

The customer in most cases will say 'Yes' to the pre-close question. If she says 'No' you are probably wasting your time.

The pre-close works because you are effectively saying, 'We accept that you have these areas of mismatch, but *if* we were at perfect match, and each of these points had been dealt with to your satisfaction, would you proceed?'

When the customer agrees, you have won the business subject to handling the points. That's Stage 5.

5. A stands for ANSWER

In this stage you carefully answer each of the customer's concerns using the following three-step sequence.

i.   Answer the point (here's where you use your objection-handling skills).

ii. Check you have answered it satisfactorily, i.e. you have fulfilled the conditional close.

iii. Cross out the point. Once it's crossed out, it's unlikely to be referred to again.

1. ~~Price~~
2. ~~Competition~~
3. ~~Delivery~~
4. ~~Support~~
5.
6.

If you cannot handle all of the points at this meeting, at least you now know exactly what remains to be done. To win the business you will have to deal with it later or gain the customer's agreement to overlook it.

Once you have dealt with everything on the list, move on to Stage 6.

6. A stands for ASK BACK

'*Are you happy that we've covered each of these points?*'

This stage double checks the customer is happy, which again conveys your intense customer focus. It's a relationship-building question.

7. C stands for CLOSE

'*Good, then we're in business.*'

You now tie up the sale in the normal way with, for example, 'Let's complete the paperwork,' or, 'Would you prefer installation this week or next?', or whatever is appropriate.

That's the LACPAAC® model. Read this appendix again and then find a willing colleague and practise each stage as a role play. If you're not comfortable with my words use your own, but do keep to the structure. Make sure you are proficient with each stage before using it with a real customer.

► The LACPAAC® Closing Model Summary & Flow Chart

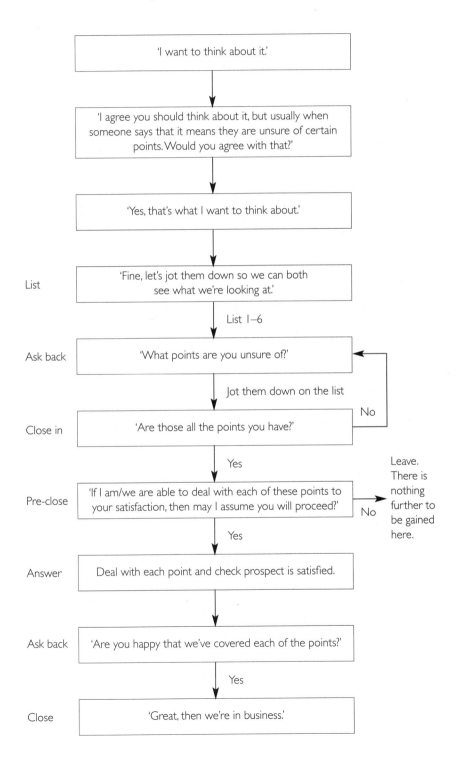

'I want to think about it.'

'I agree you should think about it, but usually when someone says that it means they are unsure of certain points. Would you agree with that?'

'Yes, that's what I want to think about.'

List — 'Fine, let's jot them down so we can both see what we're looking at.'

List 1–6

Ask back — 'What points are you unsure of?'

Jot them down on the list

Close in — 'Are those all the points you have?' — No

Yes

Pre-close — 'If I am/we are able to deal with each of these points to your satisfaction, then may I assume you will proceed?' — No — Leave. There is nothing further to be gained here.

Yes

Answer — Deal with each point and check prospect is satisfied.

Ask back — 'Are you happy that we've covered each of the points?'

Yes

Close — 'Great, then we're in business.'

About LDL Leadership Development Ltd

www.ldl.co.uk

LDL design and deliver highly structured practical training solutions and executive coaching in four main areas:

- Sales and Negotiation
- Management and Leadership
- Service Excellence
- Communication

Programmes are available as open courses, seminars or as in-company training.

If you would like to discuss which is the best route for you, our course adviser team will be delighted to help. Call us on +44(0) 20 7381 6233.

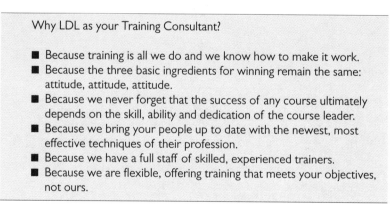

Why LDL as your Training Consultant?

- Because training is all we do and we know how to make it work.
- Because the three basic ingredients for winning remain the same: attitude, attitude, attitude.
- Because we never forget that the success of any course ultimately depends on the skill, ability and dedication of the course leader.
- Because we bring your people up to date with the newest, most effective techniques of their profession.
- Because we have a full staff of skilled, experienced trainers.
- Because we are flexible, offering training that meets your objectives, not ours.

A selection of clients for whom LDL has researched, designed and delivered in-company training solutions.

Abbey National
Abbott Laboratories
ABI Building Data
Accor Corporate Services
AGA Gas
Air Products
Alternative Networks
AMP
ARAMARK
Arthur Andersen
Ashworth Frazer
Astra Pharmaceuticals
Avaya
Baker Tilly
Bankers Trust
Barclays Bank
Barclays Capital Group
Baring Asset Management
Bass Brewers
Bayer
bioMérieux
Boston Retail Products
BPP Publishing
British Airways
British Gas
British Sky Broadcasting
BT
Bull Information Systems
BUPA
Business Objects
Cable London
CACI
Cannon Rubber
Capital Radio
Carphone Warehouse
Celltech Chiroscience
Chamber of Commerce
CISCO Systems
Clarks International
Comet Group
Compaq
CompuServe
Computacenter
Computer 2000
Co-op Travel
Co-operative Bank
Courtaulds
Daily Mail
Datamonitor
DC Cook
Dell Computer Corporation
Delphi Group
DHL International
Diesel
Dow Jones Newswires
Dun & Bradstreet
Easynet
Endress + Hauser

Energis
Energizer
EULER Trade Indemnity
Evening Standard
F&C Management
Financial Times
Fleet Street Publications
FPD Savills
Fujitsu ICL
GE Information Services
GoJobsite UK
Graduate Appointments
Granada Technology Group
Grosvenor Estate Holdings
Halifax
Hays Management
HCS Global
Hitachi Data Systems
Honda
HSBC Asset Finance UK
IIR
IKON
ING Barings
Institute of Direct Marketing
Integralis
Interval International
Jarrold Publishing
JCB Credit
JLA
JP Morgan
Keltec
Kewill
Kingston Communications
Kodak
Kuoni Travel
Lego UK
Liaison VAT Consultancy
LIFFE
Lloyds TSB
Lombard
M&G Group
MAERSK
Marsh UK
Mazda
Merrill Lynch
Mirror Group Newspapers
Misco Computer Suppliers
Moat House Hotels
Morse
Motorola ISG
National Australia Group
National Britannia Group
National Grid
Nationwide Building Society
NatWest
NFU Mutual & Avon Group
Nike
Nissan

Nomura International
Norweb
Novotel
npower
Office Angels
OKI Systems
Orange
Ovum
P&O Nedlloyd
Panorama & Manos Holidays
Pfizer
Pilkington
PKF
Powerhouse Retail
PP Payne
PricewaterhouseCoopers
Progress Software
Punter and Southall
Quest International
QVC
Racal Datacom
Radio Frequency Investigation
Random House
Reuters
Rolls Royce
Royal & Sun Alliance
  Insurance
Royal Bank of Scotland
Royce Consulting
Scottish Parliament
Scottish Power
Securicor
Sedgwick Group
Seer Technologies
SHL Systemhouse
Siemens Communications
Simmons & Simmons
Standard Life
Sterling Publications
The Environment Council
Thomas Cook Holidays
Thomson Group
Toshiba International Systems
Toyota
UBS AG
Unijet Group
University of Warwick
Virgin Direct
Virgin One Account
Volkswagen Group
Weetabix
Wella UK
Wilson Bowden
Z Card Europe
Zeneca Pharma
Zurich Scudder Investments

More than 340,000 people trained.   ISO 9001 certified

▶ Commitment to Quality

The quality of the training is constantly reaffirmed by an unusually high level of repeat business. Hundreds of companies, both large and small, keep coming back for more because they know LDL training works. At once.

Certification to the ISO 9001 quality standard, together with the Investors in People Award, provide tangible evidence of our uncompromising commitment to quality.

In a market cluttered with trainers and advice givers, LDL stands clearly above the crowd as a solid proven provider.

All LDL programmes are thoroughly researched to provide maximum learning in minimum time. We use the most up-to-date learning models, refined by on-the-job feedback, case histories, validated self-assessment inventories, skills practice, tutor presentation and varied delivery methodologies.

▶ Open Courses from LDL – High Energy Learning That Delivers

Professional Selling Skills – Three Days

This tried and tested foundation course is designed to give sales people of all levels a complete training in the modern consultative-partner skills demanded by today's market place.

The course describes sales skills in a definable, precise way. Participants learn to use questions not reasons as their main persuasive tools.

Major Account Selling – Three Days

Whatever your organisation sells it is likely that 80 per cent of your profits come from just 20 per cent of your customers. These customers are your key accounts.

This course is designed to give your sales people all the necessary skills to make LARGE sales to LARGE customers. Many companies have been transformed by their sales team learning and using these techniques.

Professional Sales Management – Three Days

How to improve the performance of each member of your sales team. And how to do it profitably. The course centres on improving sales people by combining performance improvement techniques with the correct leadership style.

Participants discover new ways to inspire greater teamwork and co-operation from others. The end result is a smoother running, more motivated, more productive sales team.

Professional Negotiating Skills – Two Days

Negotiating skills are vital. No other form of training has such an immediate measurable effect on the bottom line. Negotiation is a major factor in profitability.

This course is about commercial negotiating skills. It is designed for sales people, sales managers, key account executives and any manager involved with negotiating win-win outcomes. The course clearly defines the core of negotiation as 'both move'.

Telephone Selling – Two Days

Never before has telephone selling had such an important role in the marketplace. Its obvious cost effectiveness is making it a vital growth area. This course sets out to provide a stream of ideas to improve telephone selling skills.

Each participant leaves with a telephone technique specially developed for their business. They return to the office with all the necessary energy, enthusiasm and skill.

Making Appointments By Telephone – One Day

Making appointments with new prospects is where selling begins. In this content-rich, yet inspirational one-day course your people learn to make it a strength, not an Achilles' heel.

The programme is suitable for anyone who would like to improve his or her conversion rate, whether the challenge is cold calling, resurrecting an old database or networking with existing clients to find new business.

Finance for Non-Financial Managers – Two Days

Money is the language of business. The ability to understand and analyse financial data is essential for successful management. This course is designed to help executives come to grips with the fundamentals of finance and accounting.

The content transforms the jargon, concepts and ratios of finance into a set of straightforward business tools the non-financial manager can use every day to sharpen performance.

Effective Speaking and Presentation – Two Days

Many executives have excellent ideas. They have the enthusiasm. But when they stand up, they lose them both. This course is the solution. The emphasis throughout is on individual tuition. Video recordings are used so participants can see themselves as others see them.

In every organisation there is a critical shortage of good presenters. No skill opens more doors, creates more visibility or motivates more effectively.

▶ Seminars With Robin Fielder

Big Ticket Selling! – One Day

How to sell to major accounts. This seminar is a state-of-the-art modern sales training programme for the salesperson who sells complex products and services in a multicall, multidecision-maker environment.

Inspirational Leadership! – One Day

How to motivate, lead and inspire your people to perform at a high level on a consistent basis. Gives you the know-how to build a high-performance, high-trust culture that re-energises your people and keeps re-energising them.

Towards Peak Performance! – One Evening

Just as you increase your physical strength by lifting progressively heavier weights, it is possible in business to train your mind systematically to attain higher and higher performance levels. Not strict NLP but uses many of the principles.

Close That Sale! – One Evening

For three and a half hours after business hours and almost non-stop, you will be exposed to a stream of cutting-edge skills to develop modern selling ability. A staggering 127,000 people have attended Close That Sale! making it the biggest selling programme in UK training history.

Index

Choose Happiness

(Ten steps to bring the magic back into your life)